EPIC BATTLES
OF THE CHESSBOARD

Epic Battles

OF THE CHESSBOARD

By R. N. Coles

Edited and Revised by
FRED REINFELD AND I. A. HOROWITZ

DAVID McKAY COMPANY, INC.

New York

GV
1452
.C6
195?

Preface

I can do no better in giving my reasons for making the present collection of games than to tell the story of an incident that occurred at a British Chess Federation congress. Two moderate players were engaged in a very complicated and exciting game, and a well-known master was looking on. When the game finished in a draw, White said to Black, "I enjoyed that. It was a really good game." "Good?" interposed the master. "But White could have won a piece nine moves ago, and Black three moves later missed a forced mate in six!" The pieces were set up again, and the correctness of the master's analysis was established. "All the same it was a rattling good game," said White. A look of puzzled exasperation came over the master's face. "The mate in six, with a queen sacrifice and a knight sacrifice—that is good, yes, but you did not see it." "No," said Black, "and I never shall see things like that though I study master brilliancies till the cows come home." "Then the game is not good?" "All right," agreed Black, "it was not good, but it was the most enjoyable game I've had for months." With a helpless shrug of his expressive shoulders the master left them.

The artist is a being apart, searching ever after perfection; the rest of us can admire works of art, but we cannot create them. As with art, so with chess, the difference being that we do not leave the playing of the game to the experts; we continue to extract the utmost pleasure from the humble rough-and-tumble chess of which we are capable; and if we occasionally miss a brilliancy because our imagination will not rise to it, we probably get greater pleasure from a greater number of games than the artist does who cannot appreciate anything less than perfection. As long as a game is hard fought, and especially if it is complicated and exciting, that game is enjoyable and good enough for most of us.

Many collections of games have been made in which the

brilliancies that are beyond the average player are beautifully displayed. We admire them but cannot relate them to our own play over the board. We watch the defeated master in the ineluctable toils, but our own opponents wriggle out of our best laid schemes, and as like as not we then have to struggle to avoid defeat ourselves; we seek to attain supremacy only to find our opponent securing the ascendancy on some other part of the board. This is chess as we know it and as we have to play it.

The present collection consists of master examples of the sort of game that White and Black enjoyed so much at the congress; here may be seen how the masters react when a combination goes wrong or when their opponents fight back; in these games neither player is content to be smothered by the brilliant imagination of the other, nor to allow master technique to win a won game by copybook methods; here is complicated, fighting chess.

A few of the games will be old favorites, which could not well be omitted from a collection of this nature, but if their presence serves to whet the appetite for more like them, well and good. Many of the others will be less well known. The notes are indebted to many sources for analyses, and these have frequently passed through so many hands that it has not been possible to acknowledge the original except in a few cases; the few original notes are designed to throw into relief the up-and-down nature of the various battles.

R. N. C.

Contents

PREFACE   5

GAMES

1. McDonnell–Labourdonnais, *Match, 1834*   11
2. Labourdonnais–McDonnell, *Match, 1834*   15
3. Boncourt–Saint-Amant, *Paris, 1839*   19
4. Anderssen–Von der Lasa, *Berlin, 1851*   22
5. Bird–Horwitz, *London, 1851*   25
6. Anderssen–Morphy, *Match, 1858*   29
7. Morphy–De Rivière, *Paris, 1863*   32
8. Anderssen–Steinitz, *Match, 1866*   34
9. Zukertort–Steinitz, *Match, 1872*   38
10. Burn–Mackenzie, *Match, 1886*   42
11. Tarrasch–Gunsberg, *Frankfort, 1887*   45
12. Weiss–Tchigorin, *New York, 1889*   48
13. Taubenhaus–Tarrasch, *Nuremberg, 1892*   51
14. Pillsbury–Tarrasch, *Hastings, 1895*   54
15. Steinitz–Pillsbury, *St. Petersburg, 1896*   57
16. Pillsbury–Tchigorin, *St. Petersburg, 1896*   60
17. Charousek–Pillsbury, *Nuremberg, 1896*   63
18. Steinitz–Lasker, *World Championship Match, 1896*   67
19. Lasker–Blackburne, *London, 1899*   70
20. Janowski–Burn, *Munich, 1900*   73
21. Marshall–Pillsbury, *Vienna, 1903*   76
22. Lasker–Napier, *Cambridge Springs, 1904*   78
23. Duras–Teichmann, *Ostend, 1906*   81
24. Rubinstein–Lasker, *St. Petersburg, 1909*   85

8 CONTENTS

25. Marshall—Capablanca, *Match, 1909*   89
26. Schlechter—Lasker, *World Championship Match, 1910*   93
27. Mieses—Capablanca, *Berlin, 1913*   96
28. Capablanca—Marshall, *New York, 1918*   100
29. Rubinstein—Alekhine, *London, 1922*   103
30. Reti—Becker, *Vienna, 1923*   106
31. Znosko-Borovsky—Alekhine, *Baden-Baden, 1925*   110
32. Tartakover—Bogolyubov, *London, 1927*   112
33. Capablanca—Nimzovich, *Bad Kissingen, 1928*   116
34. Euwe—Bogolyubov, *Match, 1928*   120
35. Vidmar—Euwe, *Carlsbad, 1929*   123
36. Alekhine—Bogolyubov, *World Championship Match, 1929*   126
37. Stoltz—Colle, *Bled, 1931*   130
38. Colle—Kashdan, *Bled, 1931*   133
39. Euwe—Yates, *Hastings, 1931–32*   137
40. Spielmann—Lasker, *Moscow, 1935*   140
41. Horowitz—Trifunovich, *International Team Tournament, Warsaw, 1935* 144
42. Pleci—Fenoglio, *Mar del Plata, 1936*   147
43. Euwe—Alekhine, *World Championship Match, 1937*   150
44. Reshevsky—Botvinnik, *AVRO Tournament, 1938*   154
45. Ulvestad—Reinfeld, *Ventnor City, 1939*   158
46. Rojahn—Czerniak, *International Team Tournament, Buenos Aires, 1939* 161
47. Nyman—Sköld, *Stockholm, 1943*   163
48. Euwe—Bisguier, *New York, 1948–49*   165
49. Barden—O'Kelly, *Hastings, 1948–49*   167
50. Matanovich—Rossolimo, *Staunton Centenary Tournament, 1951*   170
Index of Openings   175

EPIC BATTLES
OF THE CHESSBOARD

GAME 1

McDonnell—Labourdonnais

MATCH, 1834

Louis Charles Mahé de Labourdonnais (1795–1840) was the greatest master of the first third of the nineteenth century, no rival worthy of him being found until 1834, when he came to London and played Alexander McDonnell (1798–1835) in a series of games that still bear comparison with those of any later age. The Frenchman won because of his greater versatility and superior position judgment. The premature death of both players was an irreparable loss, and it is fitting that they lie now in adjacent graves in Kensal Green in London.

KING'S BISHOP'S
OPENING

White	Black
McDonnell	Labourdonnais
1. P–K4	P–K4
2. B–B4	B–B4
3. P–QB3	Q–K2
4. N–B3	P–Q3

4 . . . , B×Pch.; 5 K×B, Q–B4ch.; 6 P–Q4, Q×B; 7 N×P is of dubious value for Black. The quaint opening play is typical of the times.

5. O–O	B–N3
6. P–Q4	N–KB3
7. N–R3	B–N5

7 . . . , N×P?; 8 R–K1, P–KB4; 9 B–Q5 gives Black a difficult game.

| 8. N–B2 | QN–Q2 |

8 . . . , N–B3 transposes into the Giuoco Piano! But 8 . . . , N×P?; 9 B–Q5 is bad for Black.

9. Q–Q3

There are drawbacks to the Queen's position here; 9 B–KN5 is simpler.

9.   P–Q4!?

A beautiful Pawn sacrifice that opens a phase of absorbing interest and complexity. The simplest reply is doubtless 10 B×P, for if 10 . . . , N×B; 11 P×N, P–K5; 12 Q–Q2, P×N?; 13 R–K1, etc.

10. KP×P

Not 10 QP×P?, P×B; 11 P×N, P×Q; 12 P×Q, P×N, and Black wins a piece.

Even after the text move, White must play with the greatest exactitude to avoid losing a piece.

10.	P–K5
11. Q–Q2!	P×N
12. R–K1	N–K5
13. Q–B4	P–KB4
14. P×P	P–N4!

Labourdonnais forces the

11

play with his usual inventiveness.

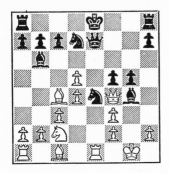

If now 15 Q×NP?, Q×Q!; 16 B×Q, B×BP, and Black remains a piece ahead: 17 R—K3, O—O! or 17 P—Q6, N—K4!

But 15 . . . , N×Q in reply to 15 Q×NP? gives White chances: 16 B×N!, Q×Rch.; 17 R×Qch., K—B1; 18 P×B, with several Pawns for the exchange.

15. Q—K3!   N—K4!!?

The complications reach an incandescent stage. Black threatens . . . , N×B or . . . , N×Pch.

16. B—N5ch.?!

Ingenious but questionable. 16 B—K2! is probably sounder.

16.   P—B3
17. P×B!

Not 17 P×P?, N×Pch., retaining the extra piece.

17.   N×NP!

Black must proceed with care. If 17 . . . , P×B?; 18 P×P winning one of the Knights with the better game.

18. Q—K2   P×B
19. P—B3!

Now it is White who must be careful. If at once 19 Q× Pch., Q—Q2:

a) 20 Q×Qch., K×Q; 21 P—B3, N—K4! 22 R—K3, N—B5, coming out the exchange ahead.

b) 20 Q—B1, Q—Q3! 21 Q—N2, B—B2!; 22 P—B3, Q×Pch.; 23 Q×Q, N×Q!; 24 K—N2, N×KBP!; 25 K×N, P—N5ch.; 26 K—N2, O—O, and Black's three connected passed Pawns should win easily for him.

19.   N/N5—B3
20. P×N   N×KP
21. Q×Pch.   Q—Q2
22. Q×Qch.   K×Q
23. P—B4

The exchange of Queens has if anything heightened the tension, as the play with the passed Pawns promises plenty of excitement.

23.   QR—K1
24. P—B5   B—Q1
25. P—Q6?

Better is 25 B—K3. Now the Bishop cannot cross to the defense of the King.

25.   P—B5!
26. P—N4   P—KR4
27. R—B1   KR—B1

28. N–R3	B–B3
29. B–N2	P–N5

For if 30 R×P?, B×Pch. The crisis is approaching.

30. N–B4	P–B6
31. N–K5ch.?	

Permitting the removal of Black's Bishop, which facilitates the advance of Black's Pawns. More logical is 31 P–N5, P–R5; 32 QR–B1 with counterplay.

31.	B×N
32. P×B	P–R5
33. QR–Q1	P–B7ch.?

Making the win difficult, not to say doubtful. The straightforward way is 33 . . . , P–N6! threatening . . . , P–N7 followed by . . . , N–N4.

34. K–R1	P–R6

With a view to 35 . . . , P–N6 (threatening mate!); 36 P×P, N×Pch., winning the exchange.

35. R–Q3	R–KN1
36. P–N5!	P–N6!
37. P×P	R×NP

Stronger than 37 . . . , N×Pch.; 38 R×N, R×R; 39 R×P, and White's Pawns compensate for the loss of the exchange.

Clearly White cannot play 38 R×R? now.

| 38. R–Q4! | |

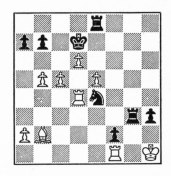

38.	R/K1–KN1?

Here 38 . . . , P–R7!! wins at once, for example 39 R×N, R–N8ch.; 40 K×P, R–R1 mate.

Or if 39 P–K6ch., R×P; 40 K×P, R–R3 mate.

By missing this incisive line, Black allows his opponent a clever drawing maneuver—which is in turn also overlooked!

| 39. P–K6ch. | |

An important factor in the defense against Black's threatened . . . , R–N8ch. Another vital function of the text move is to prevent a Black Rook from coming to KR1.

39.	K–Q1
40. R/Q4–Q1?	

Correct is 40 R×N!!, R–N8ch.; 41 K–R2! R×R (with a three-move mate threat); 42 B–B6ch., K–B1; 43 P–Q7ch., K–B2. Now White has an immediate draw with 44 B–

K5ch., etc., and there may even be winning possibilities in the position!

40.   **P–R7!**

White, it is true, can parry the threat of 41 . . . , R–N8ch.; 42 K×P, R/N1–N7ch.; 43 K–R3, N–N4ch.; 44 K–R4, R–R7 mate; but he cannot save the game.

41. **P–K7ch.**

If 41 K×P, R/N6–N3! wins.

41.	**K–Q2**
42.	**P–B6ch.**	**P×P**
43.	**P×Pch**	**K×P**
44.	**P–K8(Q)ch.**	**R×Q**
45.	**K×P**

Sooner or later, he must take the Pawn. If 45 P–Q7, R/K1–KN1; 46 P–Q8(Q), R×Q; 47 R×R, R–N8ch.; 48 K×P, R×R; 49 R–KB8, K–Q4, and wins.

However, Black's reply to the text move also decides the game.

45.		**R–K3**
46.	**R–B1ch.**	**K–N4!**

More decisive than 46 . . . , K×P; 47 KR–Q1ch., K–K2; 48 R–B7ch., K–K1; 49 B–N7, R/K3–KN3; 50 R–QN1, K–Q1, etc. It is the virtual end of a very great struggle.

47.	**P–R4ch.**	**K–N5**
48.	**B–B3ch.**	**R×B**
49.	**R×R**	**K×R**
50.	**P–Q7**	**R–Q3**
51.	**K–N2**	**R×P**
52.	**R–B1ch.**	**K–Q6**

For if 53 R–Q1ch., K–K7, etc.

53.	**K–B1**	**K–K6**

Resigns

A magnificently contested game whose errors recede into insignificance in the face of the ingenuity and fighting spirit that both of these celebrated masters display throughout.

Labourdonnais—McDonnell

QUEEN'S GAMBIT

	White	Black
	Labourdonnais	McDonnell
1.	P–Q4	P–Q4
2.	P–QB4	PxP
3.	P–K4	P–K4
4.	P–Q5	

There is nothing to be gained from 4 PxP, QxQch.; 5 KxQ, B–K3.

4.		P–KB4
5.	N–QB3	N–KB3
6.	BxP	B–B4
7.	N–B3	PxP
8.	N–KN5	O–O!?

Daring, for after 9 P–Q6ch., K–R1; 10 N–B7ch., RxN; 11 BxR, Black has nothing better than 11 . . . , PxP, though his central Pawn mass is impressive.

9.	O–O	B–Q3
10.	N–K6!?	

10 N/N5xKP is stronger. White soon finds that a Pawn on K6 exerts less pressure than one on Q5.

10.		BxN
11.	PxB	K–R1
12.	B–KN5	N–B3
13.	NxP	Q–K2
14.	K–R1	QR–Q1
15.	Q–R4	

The essentials of the position are as follows: White intends to exert pressure on the Queen side. Black has no adequate strategical counter. He therefore tries to place his pieces as aggressively as possible, in the hope of exploiting the White Queen's absence from the King side.

The clash of wills leads to exciting play, as White is confident he can capture booty on the Queen side and still have time to guard the other wing.

15.		P–QR3
16.	B–Q5!	N–Q5!?

More or less compulsory. Black's threat is now 17 . . . , P–B3; 18 B–N3, P–N4!; 19 QxRP, R–R1; 20 Q–N6, KR–QN1, trapping White's Queen!

17.	BxN	PxB
18.	BxP	QxP
19.	QR–K1	

Reluctant to accept the offer. If 19 QxP, P–KB4; 20 NxB, RxN; 21 Q–R4 (not 21 Q–R3?, N–B7, nor 21 Q–Q3, P–K5), P–K5 with a strong position.

19.		P–KB4
20.	N–B3	

Threatening 21 Q×N.

20.   Q—B3
21. Q×P?!

Better is 21 R—K3, for the attack on his King is stronger than is at first apparent.

21.   P—K5
22. Q—B4?

Now 22 R—K3 is essential. White's King side is almost denuded of protection, while Black's pieces and center Pawns are admirably posted for attack. White's carefree attitude should cost him the game.

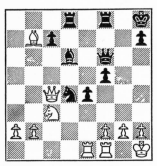

22.   B×P?!

Clever but not the best. After 22 . . . , N—B6!; 23 R—K3 (23 P×N, Q—R5, etc.), Q—R5, White is lost: 24 P—KR3, N—N4, and 25 . . . , P—B5 will be devastating.

23. R—K3!

Not 23 K×B?, Q—R5ch.; 24

K—N1, N—B6ch.!; 25 P×N, R—N1ch., followed by mate.

With the text move, White begins to fight his way out.

23.   N—B6?!

The only way to continue the attack, but 23 . . . , B—Q3 is more prudent.

24. R×N!   P×R
25. K×B   R—Q5
26. Q—B5   P×P

He cannot prevent the Bishop from returning to the defense of the King, for if 26 . . . , Q—R5ch. (or 26 . . . , R—R5ch.); 27 K—N1, R—N1; 28 B×P with a solid position.

27. B×P   R—KN1!

Threatening 28 . . . , R—R5ch.; 29 K—N1 (29 B—R3?, R×Bch.!, leads to mate), Q—N2; 30 Q—Q5, R—K5! winning.

28. P—B4?

This loses the Pawn. Better 28 B—R3 and if 28 . . . , R—KR5; 29 Q—K3, etc.

28.   Q—N2
29. R—B2   R×P
30. R—K2   R—KN5
31. B—R3   R—KB5
32. R—N2   Q—Q5

At last Black's initiative is spent. The defense has been very trying, but now White's material advantage should tell.

33. Q×Qch.   R×Q
34. R—KB2

After 34 B×P, R×Rch.; 35
K×R, R—Q7ch., White cannot
hope to win.

34.   P—B5
35. P—R4   K—N2
36. B—N2!

Envisaging the advance
and possible queening of the
Queen Rook Pawn, about
which the remaining play re-
volves. The situation calls for
desperate measures on Black's
part, and his reply prepares a
subtle plan.

36.   R—KB1
37. P—R5   R—Q3
38. B—N7?!

Stronger is 38 N—Q5!, and
if 38 . . . , P—B6; 39 R×P!,
R×N; 40 R—N3ch.! winning.

38.   R—B4
39. P—R6!   P—B6!

By this sudden counter-
attack (threatening 40 . . . ,
R—KN3, and 41 . . . , R—R4

mate, and later another mate
at KR8), Black hopes to force
40 B×P, R×P, ending the
threat on the Queen Rook file.
But his plan turns out to be
one move too late!

40. K—N1   R—N3ch.
41. K—B1   R—R3
42. K—K1   R—R8ch.
43. K—Q2   R—R8

Now Black seems to have
succeeded in his plan to halt
the Queen Rook Pawn, and is
in a position to advance his
own Pawns, which come within a hair of queening!

44. K—Q3!!

This deep but unassuming
move is a necessary preparation for yet another plan to
advance the Queen Rook
Pawn.

44.   K—B3

Hoping to induce White to
waste time capturing the
Queen Bishop Pawn while he
mobilizes King side.

45. N—Q5ch.!

Apparently accepting the
bait, but actually continuing
the plan made the previous
move to bring the Knight to
QR3 or QR5, cutting off
Black's Rook on the Queen
Rook file.

45.   K—N4
46. N—K3!   R—B3

The purpose of White's 44th

move is now clear: N—B4 cannot be prevented, whereas if only 47 N—B2 were available, Black could reply 47 . . . , R—R4, or 47 R—R5.

47. N—B4!   P—R4?

If 47 . . . , R—R5; 48 P—N3, R—R8 (more point to White's 44th; with the King on Q2, Black could now play . . . , R—R7ch.); 49 P—N4, R—R5 (aiming to get rid of both White Queen-side Pawns for the Rook); 50 K—B3, and then only N—R5.

Black therefore proceeds with his own plans, though he stood a better chance of drawing by 47 . . . , R×P!; 48 B×R, R×B; 49 R×P, P—R4, etc.

48. N—R3   R—Q8ch.
49. K—B2   R—Q1
50. P—R7   K—N5
51. P—R8(Q)   R×Q
52. B×R

White has succeeded in queening the outside passed Pawn according to schedule and is now two pieces ahead. But Black is undismayed and continues to fight on with lion-hearted courage. His Pawns are becoming increasingly dangerous.

52.   K—N6
53. R—B1   K—N7
54. R—Q1   P—B3!

Cutting off the Bishop and threatening . . . , P—B7. White is apparently in difficulties, and his next move gives the impression that the best he can do is to play 56 B—B8 and then sacrifice the Bishop for the Rook Pawn, with a draw.

55. B—N7?   P—B7
56. N—B4!   R—K3

Not 56 . . . , P—B8(Q); 57 N—K3ch. Luck or foresight?

57. N—Q2   P—R5
58. P—N4!

Finding the correct method just in time, which is to open the diagonal. (Thus White's 55th merely lost a tempo!)

58.   P—R6
59. P—N5   P—R7
60. B×Pch.   K—N6
61. B—R1   R—QN3
62. R—N1   R—N1
63. P—N6   Resigns

For after 64 N—B1ch., K—R6; 65 R—N3ch., the Pawns begin to fall. A wonderfully absorbing game!

Boncourt—Saint-Amant

PARIS, 1839

Pierre Charles Fournié de Saint-Amant (1800–1873) became the leader of French chess after the departure of Labourdonnais from France. He won a short match against Staunton in 1843 but in the big return match later in the year, which was virtually for the World Championship, he was decisively defeated. An unsuccessful appearance at the Birmingham tournament of 1858 was his only other incursion into competitive play. Boncourt was a strong French master who drew a match with Szen in 1835.

GIUOCO PIANO
(in effect)

White	Black
Boncourt	Saint-Amant
1. P–K4	P–K4
2. B–B4	N–KB3
3. P–Q3	B–B4
4. N–KB3	N–B3
5. P–B3	B–N3

The opening has turned into a Giuoco Pianissimo.

6. O–O	O–O
7. B–KN5	P–Q3
8. P–QN4	

The Queen-side advance, though it leads to critical situations for Black later on, is ultimately weakening; see Black's 30th and 31st moves.

8.	B–K3
9. QN–Q2	P–KR3
10. B–R4	K–R2!

Preparing to support a King-side attack with . . . , KR–N1 and . . . , P–N4. The immediate . . . , P–N4 can be answered by 11 N×NP!, P×N; 12 B×NP.

11. P–R4	P–R3
12. K–R1	KR–N1!
13. Q–B2	

Threatening 14 P–Q4, P×P?; 15 P–K5ch., winning a piece.

13.	P–N4!
14. B–KN3	P–KR4!
15. P–R3	

Too accommodating; 15 P–R4 is decidedly more forceful.

15.	P–R5
16. B–KR2	N–KR4
17. P–Q4	

White begins an action in the center, even at the possible cost of a Pawn, in order to divert Black from his attacking plans; thus if 17 . . . , P×P; 18 B×B, P×B; 19 P–N5, etc.

17.	P–N5!

Saint-Amant is not to be sidetracked. In the event of 18 P—Q5, he gets a strong attack with 18 . . . , P×N; 19 N×P, B×RP; 20 P×B, Q—B3; 21 Q—K2, N—K2, threatening 22 . . . , N—N6ch.!

18.	B×B	P×B
19.	RP×P	R×P
20.	P×P	P×P
21.	N—B4	N—N6ch.!

A splendid continuation, ignoring the threatened loss of the King Pawn and continuing the attack at all costs. The resulting powerful Pawn wedge at KN6 gives rise to many mating motifs.

| 22. | P×N | P×P |

Now the form of Black's attack is clear. Here are some possibilities:

a) 23 N/B4×P?, N×N; 24 N×N, R—R5; 25 N—B3, R× Bch.; 26 N×R, Q—R5, forcing mate.

b) 23 N/B3×P?, R—R5; 24 N×B, R×Bch.; 25 K—N1, R— R8ch.!; 26 K×R, Q—R5ch., and mate next move.

c) 23 N×B (best), P×N; 24 QR—Q1, Q—K2; 25 Q—Q2!, R—Q1; 26 Q—QB2, R—R5— but not 25 R—Q3, R—R1!; 26 R/B1—Q1, K—N3; 27 R—Q7, R×Bch.!; 28 K—N1, R/N5— R5! with the possible continuation 29 N×R/R4, Q×N; 30 K—B1, Q—B5ch.; 31 K—K1, Q—K6ch., and mate follows.

| 23. | QR—Q1 | Q—K2! |
| 24. | P—N5 | |

White also plays to win; he is a piece ahead and hopes to capture another while Black goes after the condemned Bishop. Nevertheless, 24 N×B is still best.

| 24. | | R—R5! |

Black carries out the attack in fine style. He now threatens 25 . . . , R×Bch.; 26 N×R, Q—R5, forcing mate.

| 25. | N×B | |

Of course not 25 P×N?, when 25 . . . , R×Bch. brings Black's attack to one of its successful conclusions.

Also ineffectual is 25 QN— Q2, R—R3!; 26 P×N, K—N2!; 27 KR—K1, QR—R1; 28 N—B1, R×Bch.! 29 N/B1×R, R× Nch.!; 30 N×R, Q—R5, forcing mate.

| 25. | | R×Bch.! |
| 26. | K—N1 | Q—B4ch.! |

A many-pointed move that has to be calculated accurately. White has escaped from one bad pin only to run into another just as bad.

27. **R—B2**

If 27 N—Q4, KP×N threatening 28 . . . , P—Q6ch., or 28 . . . , R—R8ch.!

27.   **P×N**

Not 27 . . . , P×Rch.?; 28 K×R, P×N; 29 P×N.

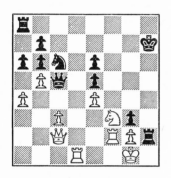

28. **N×R**

Now 28 P×N does not win a piece because 28 . . . , R—R3! followed by the capture of White's Rook leaves him the exchange down. He must therefore capture the Rook.

28.   **P×P**
29. **P×P**   **R—KB1!**
30. **N—B3**

Clearly 30 P×N?, R×R, is disastrous for White.

30.   **N—R4!**

Black brings all his pieces onto good squares before recovering the piece. He does not fear 31 N—N5ch., K—N3; 32 N×P, because of 32 . . . ,

P×Rch.; 33 K—B1, Q—B5ch., winning the Knight.

31. **Q—K2**   **N—B5!**
32. **N—N5ch.**   **K—N3**

Black is again prepared for 33 N×P, which can be answered by 33 . . . ,Q×Rch.; 34 Q×Q, P×Qch.; 35 K—B1, N—K6ch., and wins.

33. **N—B3**   **R—B5!**
34. **R—Q3**   **P×Rch.**
35. **Q×P**   **Q×Qch.**
36. **K×Q**   **R×P**

Black's passed Pawn, the dividend eked out from his brilliant attack, will win the game for him.

37. **R—Q7**   **R—B5!**
38. **R×P?**

Loses out of hand. But the game was also lost after 38 K—N3, R—B2:

a) 39 R—Q1, P—K5; 40 N—Q4, P—K4; 41 N—K6, K—B4; 42 N—Q8, R—N2ch.; 43 K—B2, P—K6ch.; 44 K—N1, P—K7; 45 R—K1, R—Q2, and the Knight is trapped.

b) 39 R×R, K×R; 40 K—N4, K—B3, threatening 41 . . . , N—Q3 with an easy win.

38.   **P—K5**
39. **K—N3**   **P×N!**

A brilliant conclusion to a tremendous game. If the Rook is captured, Black's Pawn queens.

40. **P×P**   **P—K4**
     Resigns

GAME 4

Anderssen—Von der Lasa

BERLIN, 1851

Adolf Anderssen (1818–79) did not become prominent until he was thirty years of age, but then rapidly became known as the most brilliant combinative player of his time, and was regarded as the world champion from his victory at the London tournament of 1851 until his loss of a match to Steinitz in 1866; the only break in this period of supremacy was when Morphy was playing. Among his other great victories were London, 1862, and Baden-Baden, 1870.

Tassilo von Heydebrand und der Lasa (1819–99), the most brilliant and the strongest of the German "Pleiades," was prevented after 1840 from participating in competitive play by his duties as an ambassador of the Prussian court. He always retained an interest in the game, but an unfinished series against Staunton in 1853 was his only contest of a serious nature.

KIESERITZKY GAMBIT

	White	Black
	Anderssen	Von der Lasa
1.	P–K4	P–K4
2.	P–KB4	P×P
3.	N–KB3	P–KN4
4.	P–KR4	P–N5
5.	N–K5	N–KB3

Far superior to the then customary 5 . . . , P–KR4?; 6 B–B4, R–R2, etc.

6. B–B4   Q–K2!?

An interesting deviation from the usual continuation 6 . . . , P–Q4; 7 P×P, B–N2.

After the move in the text, the following are in Black's favor: (*a*) 7 N×BP, Q×Pch.; 8 Q–K2, Q×Qch.; 9 K×Q, P–Q4; or (*b*) 7 B×Pch., K–Q1; 8 P–Q4, P–Q3; 9 B–N3,

P×N; 10 P×Pch., KN–Q2; 11 P–K6, N–B3; 12 P×N, Q× Pch., etc.

7. N×NP   N×P
8. O–O!   P–KB4!

The "to be or not to be" of Black's game pivots on his occupation of K5, which keeps the King file closed.

Von der Lasa has wisely avoided the win of a piece by 8 . . . , Q–B4ch.; 9 P–Q4, Q×B, for after 10 R×P, N–Q3 (or 10 . . . , P–Q4; 11 N–K5, Q–R3; 12 R×P, etc.), 11 P–Q5! Black is lost, despite his extra piece, because his Queen is cut off from the defense.

9. N–B2   Q×P
10. P–Q4   N–KB3

White was threatening 11 N×N, P×N; 12 R×P, etc.

If (instead of the text move) 10 . . . , B–R3; 11 N–Q2 forces Black to retreat or exchange.

11.	N–Q2	P–Q4
12.	N–B3	Q–N6
13.	R–K1ch.	B–K2
14.	Q–K2	N–B3
15.	B–N5	

Renewing the threat of checkmate!

15.		N–K5
16.	N–K5	

16.   K–B1?

Black has managed to entrench his Knight again at K5, but White's Knight at his K5 is just as powerfully posted! With his last move (which is not the best, however), Von der Lasa has avoided a bewildering variety of complications:

a) 16 . . . , N×N?; 17 N×N, N–K5; 18 N–K5ch.?, P–B3; 19 Q–R5ch., K–Q1; 20 N–B7ch., K–Q2!; 21 B×P! (if 21 Q×Pch.?, K–K1! and

Black wins), Q×B; 22 N×R, Q–B7ch.; 23 K–R2, Q–B5ch.!; 24 K–N1, Q–B7ch., drawing.

b) 16 . . . , N×N?; 17 N×N, N–K5; 18 Q–R5ch.!, K–B1; 19 Q–R6ch., with a winning position.

c) 16 . . . , Q×Nch.!; 17 Q×Q, N×Q; 18 N×N, N–K5, is quite safe for Black.

d) 16 . . . , KR–N1?; 17 N/B2–Q3! (not 17 Q–R5ch.?, R–N3!), followed by 18 B×P, favors White.

Variation *c* was therefore Black's proper course.

17.	B×N	P×B
18.	N/B2–Q3!	

A strong move. White's efforts must be concentrated on removing the weak but annoying advanced King Bishop Pawn.

18.		B–N4
19.	Q–R5	B–K3

Incomprehensible at first glance, but 19 . . . , K–N2? allows 20 R×N!, BP×R?; 21 Q–B7ch., K–R3; 22 B×P!, B×B; 23 Q–B6ch., K–R4; 24 N×Bch., winning.

20 . . . , QP×R is better (instead of 20 . . . , BP×R), but White retains a winning attack.

20.	N–N6ch.	K–N2

After 20 . . . , P×N; 21 Q×Rch., B–N1, White centralizes

with 22 Q—K5, and if 22 . . . ,
R—K1; 23 B×P!

21. **N/N6×P?**

Overcautious. Why not 21
N×R, R×N; 22 Q—B3, win-
ning the exchange *and* the
King Bishop Pawn?

21.   **B—B2**
22. **Q—B3**

22.   **Q×Q?**

Here Black falters; the loss
of K5 for his Knight will ruin
his position. After 22 . . . ,
QR—K1 White could hardly
lose; neither could he win.

23. **P×Q**   **N—Q3**
24. **N—K6ch!**

A fine move. It shows ex-
cellent position judgment in
obtaining complete sway over
the black squares.

24.   **B×N**
25. **B×B**   **QR—K1**
26. **B—B4!**   **KR—N1**
27. **K—B2**   **B—Q2**
28. **R—R1!**   **R—K2**

29. **QR—N1ch.**   **K—B1**
30. **B—R6ch.**   **K—B2**
31. **N—K5ch.**

As a result of his beautifully
timed play since the exchange
of Queens, Anderssen now
wins the exchange. Black defends tenaciously, but Anderssen conducts the ending with
consummate skill.

31.   **R×N**
32. **P×R**   **R×R**
33. **R×R**   **N—B5**
34. **P—B4!**   **P—Q5**
35. **R—N7ch.**   **K—K3**
36. **B—N5**   **N—N3**
37. **R×P**   **P—B4**
38. **P—B4!**   **P×P e.p.**

White threatened 39 R—K7
mate.

39. **P×P**   **P—B5**
40. **B—Q8!**   **N—Q4**

If 40 . . . , P—B4?; 41 R—
K7ch., K—Q4; 42 B×N wins.

41. **K—N3**   **P—R4**
42. **R—R6ch.**   **K—B2**
43. **R—R6**   **N×QBP**
44. **B×P**   **N—K5ch.**
45. **K—B3**   **P—B6**

The Queen Bishop Pawn
looks threatening, but Anderssen has a neat resource.

46. **B—Q6!**   **N×B**
47. **R×N**   **B—K3**
48. **R×B!**   **Resigns**

A spirited struggle worthy
of these great masters.

Bird—Horwitz

LONDON, 1851

B. Horwitz was one of the most eminent of the famous and brilliant school of seven German masters, known as the "Pleiades," which flourished between 1836 and 1846. He resided in England after 1845, and it was during this latter part of his career that he was associated with Kling in the compilation of their famous book of end-game studies.

H. E. Bird (1830–1908), a genial and popular British master, played regularly in international tournaments between 1851 and 1899. A player of dashing originality, his success was limited by a predilection for risky and unusual openings, his best results being first at London, 1879 and 1889; equal second at Hereford, 1885; and third at Philadelphia, 1876. He met both Morphy and Anderssen, and contested matches with Steinitz and Lasker. Against Steinitz in 1866, just after that player had become world champion, he only lost by the odd game in 17.

RUY LOPEZ

	White	Black
	Bird	Horwitz
1.	P–K4	P–K4
2.	N–KB3	N–QB3
3.	B–N5	N–B3
4.	P–Q4	N×QP?

Allowing White too much scope. 4 . . . , P×P gives Black more play.

| 5. | N×N | P×N |
| 6. | P–K5 | N–Q4 |

The Knight is now condemned to being buffeted about. 6 . . . , N–K5; 7 Q×P, N–B4, is somewhat better.

7. O–O!?

A superfluous gambit. 8 Q×P is strong and takes full advantage of Black's fourth move.

| 7. | | B–B4 |
| 8. | P–QB3 | |

8 Q–N4 forces a serious weakening in Black's King side: 8 . . . , P–KN3; 9 B–KR6, etc.

8.		P–QR3
9.	B–QB4	N–N3
10.	B–N3	

10 P×P, recovering the Pawn, is simple and good.

10.		P×P
11.	N×P	O–O
12.	N–K4	

Now and in the following moves, White plays for attack at all cost. Black defends skillfully after his initial weak play.

| 12. | | Q–K2 |

12 . . . , B—K2 is safer, but leaves Black with an unattractively cramped game.

13.   Q—R5   P—Q3

Not 13 . . . , B—Q5; 14 N—N5, P—R3; 15 N—B3, B—B4; 16 B×P! and wins.

14.	B—N5!	Q×P
15.	QR—K1	N—Q4

Black is desperate because of the threat of 16 N—B6ch. The text is an ingenious parry (if now 16 N—B6ch.??, N×N!) but should remain unavailing.

16.   N×B?!

After this move White still retains his winning prospects, but 16 Q—R4! (renewing the threat of N—B6ch.) is much more forcing.

16.   N—B3!

Black is skating on very thin ice. The point of his last move is that if now 17 R×Q, N×Q, and Black regains the piece.

17.	Q—R4!	Q×N
18.	B×N	P×B
19.	R—K3!	B—B4
20.	Q×P	B—N3
21.	R—N3?	

Too hasty. First 21 KR—K1! gives White an iron grip on the position.

21.   Q—K4!

Parrying the threat of 22 R×Bch., P×R; 23 Q×NPch., with a perpetual check.

22.   Q—R4   Q×P!

Satisfied that he can hold the threat to his Bishop, for which he has an ingenious defense prepared. The likely looking 22 . . . , KR—K1 only gives a draw after 23 P—B4, Q—K2; 24 Q—R6, Q—B1; 25 Q—N5, Q—K2 (not 25 . . . , P—R3?; 26 Q×Bch.).

23.	P—B4	Q—Q5ch.!
24.	K—R1	QR—K1
25.	Q—N5	Q—B7!!

Beautifully conceived. The Rook is to be forced off the King Knight file, so that the Queen will be left undefended and a further pin made possible on the diagonal. White cannot reply 26 R—KN1 because of 26 . . . , R—K8.

26.	R/N3—KB3	Q—Q7!
27.	P—KR4	

27.   P—B3!

This waiting move is better than 27 . . . , K–N2, which can be refuted by 28 P–R5!, R–K4!; 29 P–R6ch.!, K–N1; 30 Q–B6, R–R4ch.; 31 K–N1 (forced), R×P; 32 P–B5, and wins.

28. **P–R5**   **R–K4!**

The resource on which Black has been relying. He can hold his ground despite the fact that White has a stunning reply available.

29. **B×Pch.!!?**   **R×B**

Forced. If 29 . . . , K–N2; 30 P–R6ch.!, K×B (or 30 . . . , K–R1; 31 Q–B6 mate); 31 P×Rch. and 32 Q×Q.

30. **Q–Q8ch.**   **R–B1**

Not 30 . . . , K–N2?; 31 P×R winning the exchange.

31. **Q×Rch.!**   **K×Q**
32. **P×Rch.**   **K–N2?**

An error. After 32 . . . , K–K2!; 33 P×B, RP×P; 34 P×Pch., Q×P, Black's extra Pawns win for him.

33. **P×B**   **QP×P?**

A graver error, and strange coming from a famous endgame composer. Now the King will be entirely exposed. Black should not hope after his previous move for more than a perpetual check; in playing to win, he loses.

Correct is 33 . . . , RP×P; 34 P–K6, Q–K7; 35 R–B7ch.,

K–R3; 36 P–K7, P–Q4, and Black can hold his own.

34. **P×P**   **K×P**
35. **K–R2**   **P–K5**
36. **R–R3ch.**   **K–N3**
37. **R–N3ch**   **K–R2**

If 37 . . . , K–R4; 38 R–B8 threatening 39 R–R8 mate.

38. **R–B7ch.!**

Now it is White who avoids the draw (38 R–R3ch.).

38.   **K–R3**
39. **R–B6ch.**   **K–R4**

If 39 . . . , K–R2?; 40 R/B6–N6 threatening 41 R/N6–N4 with mating motifs.

40. **R–B8!**   **Q–Q5**

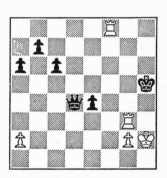

41. **R–R8ch.!**

Prettily destroying Black's position. But White's task even now presents difficulties.

41.   **Q×R**
42. **R–R3ch.**   **K–N5**
43. **R×Q**   **K–B5**
44. **R–B8ch.!?**

This is good if followed up consistently. But 44 K—N1! reduces the ending to mere technique.

| 44. | K—K6 |
| 45. | K—N3? |

Now the ending becomes a tight-rope affair. 45 K—N1 is much stronger, and so is 45 P—N4!

45.	P—B4
46. R—QN8	P—N4
47. R—N6	P—B5
48. R×RP	P—B6
49. R—QB6	K—Q7
50. K—B4	P—K6
51. R—Q6ch.	

Another winning method, which also wins by one tempo, is 51 R×P, K×R; 52 K×P, K—N7; 53 P—N4, etc.

| 51. | K—K7 |

If White had played 45 K— N1, and 50 K—B1, Black would be forced into 51 . . . , K—B7, when 52 K—K2 wins easily.

52. P—N4	K—B7
53. R—KR6!	P—K7
54. R—R2ch.	K—B8
55. K—B3!	

The saving clause and a pretty one. If now 55 . . . , P—K8(Q) or 55 . . . , P—B7; 56 R—R1 mate.

| 55. | P—K8(N)ch. |
| 56. K—K3 | N—N7ch. |

Or 56 . . . , P—B7; 57 R—R1ch., K—N2; 58 R×N, etc.

57. R×N	K×R
58. P—N5	P—N5
59. K—Q3	Resigns

A cut-and-thrust game of exceptional brilliancy throughout.

GAME 6

Anderssen—Morphy

MATCH, 1858

Paul Morphy (1837–84), the greatest master of the open game, has claims to be regarded as the greatest player of all time. His career was limited almost entirely to the years 1857 to 1859, in which time he defeated every player he met including Anderssen, Lowenthal, and Harrwitz. In style he was sound and deep but capable of exceptional brilliance when opportunity offered. After a meteoric career, he retired completely, being afflicted with a form of melancholia.

RUY LOPEZ

White	Black
Anderssen	Morphy
1. P–K4	P–K4
2. N–KB3	N–QB3
3. B–N5	P–QR3

Introducing for the first time the defense now named after him.

4. B–R4	N–B3
5. P–Q3	

Lines involving P–B3 and P–Q4 were only developed later.

5.	B–B4
6. P–B3	P–QN4
7. B–B2	P–Q4

Considered premature by most critics, this move is typical of Morphy's predilection for open positions.

8. P×P	N×P
9. P–KR3	O–O
10. O–O	P–R3
11. P–Q4?!	

Anderssen prepares to attack along the diagonal. The diagonal could be opened without allowing an isolated Pawn by 11 N×P, N×N; 12 P–Q4, but the Pawn is a bait in Anderssen's plan.

11.	P×P
12. P×P	B–N3
13. N–B3	N/Q4–N5
14. B–N1	

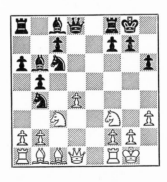

14.	B–K3

Refusing to be tempted, for 14 . . . , B×P? loses: 15 N–

K2, B—N3; 16 P—R3, N—Q4;
17 Q—B2!

14 . . . , N×QP is feasible,
but after 15 N×N, B×N (not
15 . . . , Q×N?; 16 Q—B3!,
B—K3; 17 P—R3, N—Q4; 18
R—Q1); 16 Q—B3, B—K3; 17
Q—K4, White has a very
dangerous attack. Zukertort
has shown that Black can
probably just weather it, but
over the board it would be a
dangerous venture.

| 15. | P—R3 | N—Q4 |
| 16. | N—K2 | |

Threatening 17 Q—B2.
The alternative 16 N×P is
answered by 16 . . . , N—B3;
17 N—B3, N×P.

16.		N—B3
17.	B—K3	R—K1
18.	N—N3	B—B5

Morphy has maneuvered
himself into a position where
the isolated Pawn can be captured with impunity, for if 19
R—K1, N×P; 20 N×N, B×N;
21 B×B, R×Rch.; 22 Q×R,
Q×B.

White therefore takes his
courage in both hands and
sacrifices the exchange. The
only alternative was 19 B—Q3,
renouncing his attacking aims.

19.	N—B5?!	B×R
20.	Q×B	N—K2
21.	N/B3—R4	N×N
22.	N×N	Q—Q2
23.	B×P?!	

The counterattack begins to
gather weight, but Black has
a winning reply in the simple
23 . . . , B×P!

| 23. | | P×B |
| 24. | Q—B1 | |

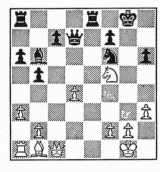

| 24. | | B×P? |

What was good a moment
earlier, is now inferior, and on
such small nuances do success
and failure so often depend.
The correct line, given by
Zukertort, was 24 . . . , N—
R2!; 25 Q×RP, P—KB3; 26
B—R2ch. (or 26 N—R4, R—
K8ch.; 27 K—R2, R×B), K—
R1; 27 N—R4, R—KN1; 28
B×R, K×B.

Even so, Morphy's line is
not obviously inferior by any
means.

25.	Q×RP	R—K8ch.
26.	K—R2	N—K5
27.	B×N!	

And it is only this brilliant
continuation that shows up
the weakness of Black's 24th
move.

27.   R×B

If 27 . . . , R×R White can
force a draw by 28 N—K7ch.,
Q×N; 29 B—R7ch., or he can
play an ending with two minor
pieces against a Rook after
28 N×B, Q—Q3ch.; 29 Q×Q,
P×Q; 30 B×R.

Once again the simple text
move seems to leave White no
future.

28.   **Q—N5ch.**   **K—B1**
29.   **Q—R6ch.**   **K—K1**
30.   **N×B!**

And once again White finds
a surprise move to keep his
game alive.

30.   **Q—Q3ch.**

30 . . . , R×N? loses after
31 R—K1ch.
If 30 . . . , Q×N; 31 Q—
B6ch., K—K2; 32 Q×QR with
a probable draw.

31.   **Q×Q**   **P×Q**
32.   **R—Q1!**   **K—B1**

Black has fought his way
through all White's brilliancies
into an ending where he is the
exchange ahead, only to find
that White can nevertheless
hold everything.

33.	R—Q2	QR—K1
34.	P—KN4	R/K1—K4
35.	P—B3	R—K8
36.	P—KR4	R—Q4
37.	K—N3	P—R4
38.	P—R5	K—N1
39.	K—B2	R—K1
40.	K—N3	K—R2
41.	K—B4	R—K2
42.	K—N3	P—B3
43.	K—B4	R—K1
44.	K—N3	R—K2
	Drawn	

Black has no target for his
Rooks and he cannot play
. . . , K—R3 because of N—
B5ch. Equally White can do
nothing with his King-side
Pawns so long as Black sits
tight.

Morphy—De Rivière

PARIS, 1863

Jules Arnous de Rivière (1830–1905), a leading French master of his day, is described by Sergeant in his Morphy book in these terms: "One of Morphy's most ardent admirers and most frequent opponents in Europe ... his most notable achievement later was a defeat of Tchigorin, 1885 (5-4-1)."

RUY LOPEZ

	White	Black
	Morphy	De Rivière
1.	P–K4	P–K4
2.	N–KB3	N–QB3
3.	B–N5	N–B3
4.	O–O	P–Q3

The defense later popularized by Steinitz and named after him.

5.	P–Q4	PXP
6.	NXP	B–Q2
7.	BXN	PXB
8.	N–QB3	B–K2
9.	P–KR3	

The opening play has been amazingly modern, but here 9 Q–Q3 or 9 P–QN3 is more effective.

9.		P–B4
10.	KN–K2	O–O
11.	P–B4	B–B3
12.	N–N3	N–Q2

Hoping to take the sting out of White's inevitable P–K5.

| 13. | Q–Q3 | R–N1 |
| 14. | P–N3 | B–B3 |

15.	B–Q2	B–Q5ch.
16.	K–R1	P–N3
17.	QR–K1	Q–R5!
18.	QN–K2	B–KN2
19.	P–B4	N–B3

Black misses a good chance here in 19 . . . , P–B4!

20.	N–B3	B–Q2
21.	KN–K2	N–R4
22.	K–R2	P–B4

Now this is not so effective.

23.	P–K5!	B–QB3
24.	P–N3	Q–Q1
25.	P–K6!?	R–K1
26.	N–KN1	

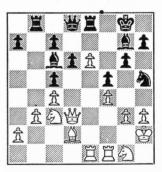

| 26. | | Q–B1 |

After 26 . . . , B×N; 27 B×
B, Black has two continuations that are only superfi-
cially inviting: (a) 27 . . . ,
B–K5; 28 R×B!, P×R; 29 Q×
KP, and White has a strong
attack; (b) 27 . . . , N–N2;
28 P–K7!, Q–Q2; 29 B–B6!

27.	N–Q5	N–B3
28.	B–B3	N×N
29.	B×B	N×P?

29 . . . , K×B is simpler and
should hold the game.

30.	R×N	K×B
31.	Q–B3ch.	K–N1
32.	P–K7!	Q–R3

Now the Queen is out of
play, but 32 . . . , B–K5; 33
R/K1×B!, P×R; 34 Q–B6,
also leaves White with a winning game.

| 33. | R–K2 | K–B2 |
| 34. | P–KN4? | |

The King Pawn has led a
charmed life and should now
be ·preserved by 34 Q–K3!
leading to a much faster win
than after the text move.

34.		R×KP
35.	R×Rch.	K×R
36.	Q–N7ch.	K–Q1
37.	Q–N8ch.	

[*See diagram in next column.*]

| 37. | | K–Q2!? |

A desperate try, as 37 . . . ,
B–K1; 38 R–B2, Q–B1; 39
P×P, leaves White with an
easy win.

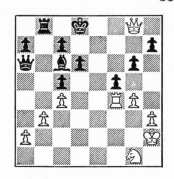

| 38. | Q×Pch.! | |

But not 38 Q×R?, Q×Pch.;
39 K–N3, P–N4!; 40 R–B2,
P–B5ch., etc.

38.		K–B1
39.	R–B2	P×P
40.	P×P	B–K5

His King Knight Pawn is
doomed.

41.	Q–K7	Q–B3
42.	R–K2	P–Q4?
43.	P×P	B×P
44.	N–R3	K–N2
45.	N–B4	R–R1ch.

White is still not out of the
woods.

46.	K–N3	B–R8
47.	R–K3	P–N4
48.	Q×NP	Q–QR3
49.	Q×P	Q×P

Despite his stubborn resistance, Black is steadily losing
ground.

| 50. | Q–N5ch.! | K–R1 |
| 51. | R–K8ch.! | R×R |

52.	Q×Rch.	K—N2
53.	Q—N5ch.	K—B1

Now White's passed Pawn has the last word.

54.	P—N5	P—B3
55.	Q—B5ch.!	K—N2
56.	Q—B7ch.!	K—N3
57.	P—N6	Q—Q7
58.	P—N7	Q—K8ch.

Black fights on to the bitter end—but White's King has a haven at QB8!

59.	K—N4	Q—N8ch.
60.	K—B5	Q—B4ch.
61.	K—B6	Q—Q5ch.
62.	K—K7	Q—B4ch.
63.	K—Q7	Q—Q5ch.
64.	K—B8	Resigns

A great fighting game.

GAME 8

Anderssen–Steinitz

MATCH, 1866

Wilhelm Steinitz (1836–1900), a Bohemian Jew, was world champion from 1866 to 1894 and the first great master of position play. He was an outstanding match player, and besides winning against Anderssen, he won, among others, three matches against Blackburne, two against Zukertort, two against Tchigorin, one against Mackenzie, and one against Gunsberg; he was finally beaten by Lasker. His tournament record, though slightly less impressive, included first prizes at London, 1871; Vienna, 1873; and New York, 1894; an equal first at Vienna, 1882; and second prizes at Dundee, 1867; Baden-Baden, 1870; London, 1883; and St. Petersburg, 1896.

EVANS GAMBIT

White	Black
Anderssen	Steinitz
1. P—K4	P—K4
2. N—KB3	N—QB3
3. B—B4	B—B4
4. P—QN4	B×P
5. P—B3	B—B4
6. P—Q4	P×P
7. O—O	P—Q6

7 . . . , P×P (a kind of Compromised Defense), though possibly playable, leads to too difficult a game for over-the-board play. The text move has the advantage that White is denied the square QB3 for his Knight, a form of development that seems essential if White is to attack.

8. **Q×P**

More energetic is 8 N—N5,
N—R3; 9 N×BP, N×N; 10 B×
Nch., K×B; 11 Q—R5ch., P—
N3; 12 Q×B, P—Q3; 13 Q—
Q5ch., B—K3; 14 Q×P/Q3,
and White has the initiative.

8.	**P—Q3**
9. **B—KN5**	**KN—K2**
10. **QN—Q2**	**P—KR3**
11. **B—R4**	**O—O**
12. **N—N3**	**B—N3**
13. **P—KR3**	**B—K3**
14. **QR—Q1**	

To prevent . . . , P—Q4.
Despite his lackadaisical
eighth move, Anderssen has
managed to secure some pressure for the offered Pawn.

14.	**Q—Q2**
15. **B—Q5**	**N—N3**
16. **B—N3**	**QR—K1**
17. **P—B4**	**B×B**
18. **KP×B**	**QN—K4**
19. **N×N**	**N×N**
20. **Q—QB3**	**N—N3**

White was threatening to
win a piece with 21 P—B5.

21. **P—B5!**

White has slightly the better development for his Pawn
and now starts an ingenious
attack that turns a material
disadvantage into a material
advantage.

21.	**P×P**
22. **N×P**	**Q—B4**

If 22 . . . , B×N; 23 Q×B,
R—B1 (not 23 . . . , R—K2;

24 P—Q6!, P×P; 25 B×P); 24
Q×RP.

23. **N×P**   **R—K7**

Both players go all out for
attack; Black allows White to
win a Pawn on the Queen side
rather than indulge in difficult
and elaborate defensive measures.

24. **P—Q6**	**P×P**
25. **N×P**	**Q—K3**
26. **P—QR4**	**B—Q1!**

If 26 . . . , P—QR4; 27 N—
N5, threatening 28 R—Q6.

27. **Q—B5**   **P—B4!**

Beginning a remarkably ingenious attack that excited the
admiration of Staunton, who
commented that Steinitz "ex-
hibits a power of combination
and a fertility of resource
which his most fervent sup-
porters had not supposed him
to possess."

And Gottschall, in his Anderssen book, writes: "The
way in which Steinitz now
exploits his advantage is beyond praise. Of all the games
of the match, this one reveals
his exceptional powers in the
most brilliant light."

28. **Q×RP**	**P—B5!**
29. **B—R2**	**N—R5!**
30. **Q—N7**	**Q—N3!**

Setting up a mating threat
that ties White's Queen to the
diagonal.

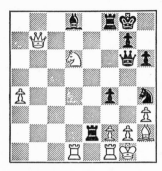

31. R—Q4?

The position is extremely critical now owing to Black's mating threat. The text move proves to be mere loss of time that puts the Knight in chancery.

However, the alternative 31 Q—Q5ch. is not entirely satisfactory after 31 . . . , K—R1 (not 31 . . . , K—R2; 32 Q—Q3); 32 N—B7ch., K—R2; 33 Q—Q3, R—K5; 34 P—N4, B—K2 (if 34 . . . , P×P e.p.; 35 B×P or 35 . . . , R×N; 36 Q×B, etc.); 35 N—Q6, B×N; 36 Q×B, N—B6ch.; 37 K—R1, R—B3; 38 Q—Q7, N—K4; 39 Q—N5, P—KR4; for White's extra Pawn is of less value than Black's attacking chances.

31.   B—N3!

The Bishop is immune from capture, as White's Queen must guard KN2. At the same time, the Bishop plays an important attacking role.

32. R/Q4—Q1

32 R—N4 allows 32 . . . , B×Pch.!; 33 R×B, R×R; 34

K×R, Q×N, with advantage to Black. And 32 R×P? is met by 32 . . . , R×P!!

32.   R—K3!

Now White's troubles are severe, for if 33 N—N5, R—QB3; 34 P—N3, P×P; 35 B×P, Q×Bch., etc.

White therefore offers the Queen Rook Pawn to draw the Black Bishop off the dangerous diagonal.

33. P—R5!   B—B4!
34. P—R6!

Black is not to be drawn, but now White has a chance of utilizing his Pawn that he seizes in splendid style. If in reply 34 . . . , B×N; 35 P—R7, R—K2; 36 P—R8(Q) winning.

34.   R—K2!

The thrusts and counterthrusts are most exciting. Black delays the capture of the Knight until he has attended to the threat of P—R7, White being always hampered by the necessity of keeping his Queen on the long diagonal.

35. Q—Q5ch.   K—R1
36. P—R7!

White still cannot rescue his Knight because of the answer 36 . . . , R—Q2!, forcing the Queen off the diagonal. He therefore sacrifices the Queen Rook Pawn in order to break out of Black's grip.

36.	B×P

If 36 . . . , R×P; 37 KR—K1, B×N; 38 R—K6, Q×Pch.; 39 Q×Q, N×Q; 40 R/K6×B, N—R5; 41 R—Q8, and the threat to Black's Bishop Pawn enables White to draw.

37.	KR—K1	R×Rch.
38.	R×R	

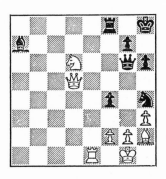

38.	K—R2!!

A move as subtle as White's defense has been fine. He sees that the forced exchange of Queens is imminent and evolves a plan to continue the attack without the Queen; the immediate threat of . . . , R—Q1 is only subsidiary to his real plan.

39.	Q—K4	R—B3
40.	N—N5	R—K3!

The point, temporarily giving up the Bishop. The play on both sides is most brilliant.

41.	Q×Qch.	R×Q
42.	N×B	R×Pch.
43.	K—R1	R×Bch.

44.	K×R	N—B6ch.
45.	K—N2	N×Rch.
46.	K—B1	N—Q6
47.	N—B6	

Now follows a difficult Knight and Pawn end game in which it is somewhat doubtful whether Black's extra Pawn is sufficient to win.

47.	K—N3
48.	K—K2	N—B4
49.	K—B3	N—K3
50.	N—K5ch.	K—B4
51.	N—Q3?	

A serious error, for the Knight is soon reduced to abject helplessness. After 51 N—B4 it would retain its freedom of action. From this moment, White's chances of saving the game vanish.

51.	P—N3
52.	N—K1	N—Q5ch.
53.	K—N2	K—K5
54.	K—B1	P—B6

Now we see the injurious effects of White's 51st.

55.	K—N1	P—N4
56.	K—R2	P—R4
57.	K—N3	N—B4ch.
58.	K—R2	P—N5
59.	P×P	P×P
60.	K—N1	

Even now White's Knight cannot come back into play, for if 60 N—B2, K—Q6; 61 N—N4ch., K—K7; 62 K—N1, P—N6! winning.

60.	K—Q5
61.	N—B2ch.	K—Q6
62.	N—R3	

Atkins has shown that no better is 62 N—N4ch. because of 62 . . . , K—K7; 63 N—Q5, P—N6; 64 N—B4ch., K—K8; 65 N—N2ch., P×N; 66 P×P, N—K6; 67 P—N4, K—K7!; 68 P—N5, K—B6; 69 P—N6, N—B4, winning.

62.   P—N6
63. N—N5

Or 63 P×P, K—K7, etc. A remarkable ending!

63.   P—N7
    Resigns

For after 64 K—R2, N—Q5! forces the game. 65 N×N, K×N leaves Black with an easy win, while avoidance of the exchange allows 65 . . . , N—K7, and the Pawn queens.

"A wonderfully interesting struggle," says Sergeant, "of which the memory ill deserves the neglect that has befallen it."

GAME 9

Zukertort—Steinitz

MATCH, 1872

Johannes H. Zukertort (1842–88) was a Pole who lived in England from 1871 on. He was a very gifted and very brilliant player but of a nervous temperament and indifferent stamina. He scored quite remarkable wins in tournament play, including first prizes at the great tournaments at Paris, 1878, and London, 1883; second prize at Berlin, 1881; and equal second at Leipzig, 1877. He was for a long time regarded as Steinitz's only great rival, but in their two great matches, in 1872 and 1886, his staying powers proved insufficient. He never understood why he failed to win.

GIUOCO PIANO

White	Black
Zukertort	Steinitz
1. P—K4	P—K4
2. N—KB3	N—QB3
3. B—B4	B—B4
4. P—B3	N—B3
5. P—Q4	P×P
6. P×P	B—N3?

Allowing White to overrun his position with 7 P—Q5, N—K2; 8 P—K5, when Black's game is hopelessly compromised. 6 . . . , B—N5ch. is the only playable move.

| 7. O—O? | N×KP |
| 8. R—K1 | O—O |

Even more unfavorable is

8 . . . , P–Q4; 9 B×P, Q×B; 10 N–B3, as Black's King is then still in the center.

9.	R×N	P–Q4
10.	B×P	

10 B–KN5 is a strong alternative.

10.		Q×B
11.	N–B3	Q–Q1
12.	P–Q5	N–K2
13.	B–N5	P–KB3
14.	Q–N3!	

White has come out of the opening with a strong initiative, and the force of his attack begins to be revealed.

The simplest reply is 14 . . . , K–R1, avoiding all complications on the dangerous diagonal. But Steinitz allows the attack to continue in the belief that the pressure cannot be maintained.

14.		R–B2

If 14 . . . , P×B; 15 P–Q6ch., R–B2; 16 P×N, Q–K1; 17 N×P, B–KB4; 18 R–K5, and White's attack nets him the win of the exchange.

15.	QR–K1!	K–B1

Not 15 . . . , P×B?; 16 P–Q6!, regaining the piece with a terrific attack.

It looks now as if White's attacked Bishop must retreat, whereupon Black can gain further time with . . . , B–KB4. Instead, Zukertort embarks on an ingenious attack which calls for the most re-

sourceful patience on the part of Steinitz.

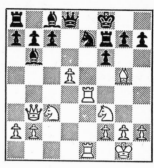

16. P–Q6!

Continuing the attack with unabated energy. If 16 . . . , Q×P?; 17 R–Q1 wins because of the mating threat on Q8.

16.		P×P
17.	N–Q5!	N×N!

Not 17 . . . , P×B; 18 R×N, R×R; 19 N×R (threatening 20 Q–N8 mate), and wins. Black's situation continues to be precarious.

18.	Q×N	

But not 18 R–K8ch.?, Q×R; 19 R×Qch., K×R; 20 Q×N, P×B, when Black has two Rooks and a minor piece for the Queen—and 21 N×P? is refuted by 21 . . . , R×P.

After the text move, White threatens 19 Q×Pch.!, Q×Q; 20 R–K8 mate.

18.		B–Q2

Black has nothing better than to sacrifice the Queen Pawn, for 18 . . . , B–QB4 is answered by 19 N—K5!, R—B2; 20 R—KB4, threatening 21 R×Pch.!, P×R; 22 B—R6ch., followed by a quick mate.

Or if 18 . . . , B—B2; 19 R—K8ch., Q×R; 20 R×Qch., K×R; 21 B—B4, with severe pressure on Black's position.

| 19. | Q×Pch. | K—N1 |
| 20. | N—K5? | B×Pch.! |

This counterattack—just in time—is very pretty, and proves that White overshot the mark with his last move.

21. K—R1

If 21 K×B, P×Nch.; 22 K—N1, Q×B wins.

21.		B×R
22.	N×R	K×N
23.	Q—Q5ch.	K—N3!!

The key move of Black's defense. 23 . . . , K—B1? fails against 24 B—B4 threatening 25 B—Q6 mate!

24. R×B   B—B3?

But now, after a superbly patient defense, Steinitz misses the best line and thus fails to refute White's faulty 20th move. 24 . . . , P×B! can at last be played, for if 25 R—Q1, R—B1! holds the extra piece because of the back-rank mating threat.

| 25. | Q×Q | R×Q |
| 26. | B—K3 | |

The Bishop has been *en prise* for twelve moves, but the time has come to with-

draw it at last. Black has emerged from his hammering a Pawn ahead, but the Bishops on opposite colors indicate a probable draw.

26.		K—B2
27.	K—N1	P—KN4
28.	R—K2	P—QR3
29.	R—Q2	R—K1

An exchange of Rooks would be a surrender of his last chance of winning; and sure enough White makes an error on his very next move, allowing Black to win another Pawn or force the Bishops off.

30.	K—B2?	B×P!
31.	B×P	P×B
32.	K×B	K—B3
33.	K—B3	P—KR4
34.	P—KR4!	

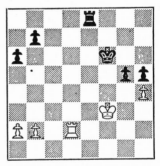

Undismayed by his previous errors, Zukertort begins to fight the ending tenaciously and devises some promising drawing possibilities.

34.   P×P

34 . . . , P—N5ch. looks right, but after 35 K—B4, it is

difficult for Black to make progress. On the other hand, after the text move, his King-side Pawns greatly depreciate in value.

35.	R—Q4	K—N4
36.	R—Q5ch.	K—N3
37.	R—Q6ch.	K—B4
38.	R—Q4	

If 38 R—Q5ch., R—K4. Black's King has therefore advanced one rank as a result of the maneuver of the last three moves.

38.		P—R6
39.	R—KR4	K—N4
40.	R×P	P—R5
41.	K—B2	

The only move to get the Rook back into play, for if 41 R—R2, R—B1ch.; 42 K—N2, K—N5.

41.		R—B1
42.	R—N3	R—B7ch.
43.	K—N1	P—N4
44.	P—R4!	

The second Rook Pawn to be sacrificed.

44.		P×P
45.	R—N4	R—B8ch.
46.	K—R2	R—QN8
47.	R×QRP	R×Pch.

48.	K—R3	R—N6ch.
49.	K—R2	R—N3
50.	K—R3	K—B4?

Surely an amazing lapse of judgment. The simple 50 . . . , R—R3 ties down White's King, so that Black's King can cross to the Queen side and force the win comfortably. After 50 . . . , R—R3 White can resign at once.

51.	K×P	R—N3
52.	K—R5	R—K3
53.	R—R5ch.	K—K5
54.	K—N5?	

"The equalizing injustice of chess"!

Apparently White can draw with 54 K—N4!, R—N3ch.; 55 K—R5, R—QB3; 56 K—N4, K—Q5; 57 K—B4, K—B5; 58 K—K3!, K—N5; 59 R—R5, P—R4; 60 K—Q2, for example: 60 . . . , P—R5; 61 R—R8, P—R6; 62 R—N8ch., K—R5; 63 R—R8ch., K—N6; 64 R—N8ch., K—R7; 65 R—QR8, K—N7; 66 R—N8ch., K—R8; 67 R—QR8, P—R7; 68 R—QN8, etc.

| 54. | | R—K4ch. |

Resigns

The exchange of Rooks naturally leaves Black with an easy win.

Burn—Mackenzie

MATCH, 1886

George H. Mackenzie (1837–91) was a Scotsman who emigrated to New York in 1863 and became an American citizen. He was an exceptionally brilliant player, and besides being American champion for many years, frequently played in European master tournaments. His best results were first at Frankfort, 1887, and second at Bradford, 1888.

Amos Burn (1848–1925) was one of the finest of all British masters, though his quiet, unobtrusive style caused him to be overshadowed in the public imagination. Between 1870 and 1887 he played only in England, but scored a continuous run of first prizes. Afterward competing abroad also, he was strikingly successful, his best results being first prizes at Amsterdam, 1889, and Cologne, 1898; and second at Breslau, 1889.

QUEEN'S PAWN GAME

	White	Black
	Burn	Mackenzie
1.	N–KB3	P–Q4
2.	P–Q4	N–KB3
3.	P–K3	P–K3
4.	P–QN3	P–B4
5.	B–N2	N–B3
6.	QN–Q2	

In modern times this line of play has become obsolete because of the continuation 6 . . . , B–Q3; 7 B–Q3, Q–K2; 8 N–K5 (else Black frees himself with . . . , P–K4), P×P; 9 P×P, B–R6.

6.		P×P
7.	P×P	B–Q3
8.	B–Q3	B–Q2

8 . . . , P–QN3 followed by . . . , B–N2 gives a more promising game. As play proceeds, White's ensuing Queen-side majority has a smothering effect on Black's position.

9.	O–O	QR–B1
10.	P–B4	O–O

10 . . . , P×P is somewhat better.

11.	R–K1	N–K2
12.	P–B5	B–N1
13.	P–QN4	N–N3
14.	P–QR4	N–B5

In view of White's decision to advance his Queen-side majority, Black seeks to provoke a target for his own attack on the other wing.

15.	B–KB1	P–KR3
16.	P–N5	N–R2
17.	P–N3	

He has no objection to falling in with Black's plan since his white squares can be protected by his Bishop.

17.		N–N3
18.	B–Q3	P–B4
19.	R–K2	N–B3
20.	N–K1	N–K5
21.	P–B4!?	

As the sequel indicates, White can weather the storm that is provoked by this move. But 21 P–B3! is certainly simpler, especially since after 21 . . . , N×N; 22 Q×N, Black cannot play 22 . . . , P–B5.

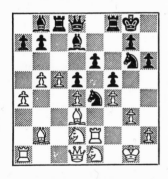

| 21. | | B×BP!? |

So far White has had decidedly the best of it and is now ready to resume his Queen-side operations. Black must therefore adopt fighting tactics if he is to have any counterchances.

| 22. | P×B | N×KBP |
| 23. | N/Q2–B3 | |

If 23 R–K3, Q–N4ch.; 24 K–B1 (24, K–R1??, N–B7

mate), Q–R5; 25 R–B3, Q× P (threatening . . . , Q–R8 mate); 26 B×N, BP×B with a tremendous attack.

| 23. | | N×Rch. |
| 24. | Q×N | B–K1 |

The Bishop lurks in the background, waiting for a chance to go into action— eighteen moves later!

| 25. | B–B1 | |

To prevent . . . , Q–N4ch. in reply to his intended N–K5.

| 25. | | P–N4 |
| 26. | N–K5 | Q–B3 |

Black is now "threatening" 27 . . . , N–B6; 28 Q–QB2, R×P!?; 29 P×R, Q×N; 30 N– N2, N–K7ch.; 31 B×N, Q×R, and though some preparatory moves to strengthen Black's game may be preferable first, the mere possibility of such a variation indicates the value of White's next move.

27.	R–R3!	K–R2
28.	B–B2	KR–N1
29.	N–N2	R–N2
30.	B–N2	P–KR4
31.	P–R5	P–R5
32.	N–K3	

So that after 33 P–R6, P×P; 34 R×P, he threatens 35 N× QP.

32.		K–N1
33.	P–R6	P–N5
34.	P×P	R×NP
35.	B–Q3	N–N4
36.	R–R6	

Even better is 36 Q—B1, and after 36 . . . , N—R6ch., Black cannot play 37 . . . , N—B5. The game now becomes most exciting.

36.		N—R6ch.
37.	K—R1	N—B5
38.	Q—Q2	N×B
39.	N×QP!	

Just in time. After 39 Q×N, B×P; 40 N×QP, B×Q; 41 N× Qch., K—N2; 42 N×B, K×N, Black gets a good game.

| 39. | | Q—N2! |

Not 39 . . . , Q—Q1?; 40 R—Q6, B—Q2; 41 N×B, R×N (or 41 . . . , P×N; 42 N—B6ch.); 42 R×R, Q×R; 43 N—B6ch., winning the Queen.

40. R×KP!

Another fine move, giving up a piece to carry on the attack. 40 . . . , B×P? is now prevented by the reply 41 R—KN6.

| 40. | | N×N |
| *41.* | *N—B6ch.!* | *K—B2* |

If 41 . . . , K—B1; 42 P×N, B×P; 43 Q—Q6ch., K—B2; 44 Q—Q5, transposing back into the game.

42. P×N!   *B×P!*

Not 42 . . . , K×R?; 43 Q— Q5ch., K—K2; 44 Q×Rch., K— B1; 45 Q×R, winning.

| *43.* | *Q—Q5* | *K—B1* |
| *44.* | *P—B6!* | *Q—N4!!?* |

Defense is no longer to be considered, and counterattack is his only chance. The text move threatens 45 . . . , Q—K6 with a view to 46 . . . , Q— K8ch., and 47 . . . , P—R6 mate.

45. R—K8ch.!

After 45 P×R?, R—B8ch.! wins:

a) 46 K—N2, P—R6ch.; 47 K—N3, P—B5ch., or 47 K—B2, Q—B5ch., with mate next move in either case.

b) 46 B×R, Q×Bch.; 47 K— N2, Q—B8 mate.

| *45.* | | *R×R* |
| *46.* | *B—R3ch.?* | |

Missing his chance. 46 P×R! can now be played:

a) 46 . . . , Q—K6; 47 Q— N8ch., K—K2; 48 N—Q5ch., K—Q2 (if 48 . . . , K—Q1; 49 P—N8[Q]ch.); 49 Q×Rch. winning easily.

b) 46 . . . , Q×N; 47 B— R3ch.! K—N2; 48 P×Qch.— but not 47 P×Q?, R—K8ch.; 48 K—N2, R—K7ch.; 49 K—B1,

R—K4ch.; 50 K—B2, R—K7ch., and Black draws.

46.		K—N2
47.	N×Rch.	K—R1
48.	P×R	Q—K6

Black has taken a long chance, and it has come off. White's reply is forced, for if 49 Q—N2, Q—K8ch.; 50 Q—

N1, B—B3ch., leading to mate.

49.	B—B5	Q—B8ch.
50.	B—N1	B—B3

White has no time now to queen the Pawn. A grand fight, even if Black was lucky.

51.	N—B6	B×Qch.
52.	N×B	Q—N8
		Resigns

GAME 11

Tarrasch—Gunsberg

FRANKFORT, 1887

Siegbert Tarrasch, despite his failure to win the world title from his compatriot Lasker, remains one of the greatest of all chess players. His tournament record from 1883 to 1914 is studded with prizes, and even to an advanced age he remained a dangerous competitor in international tournaments. His style, based on that of Steinitz, was simpler and more logical, if less imaginative. His crystallization of Steinitz's theories into precise dogmas made him one of the greatest of chess teachers and profoundly influenced the strategical appreciation of later players.

Isidor Gunsberg (1845–1930), a Hungarian, spent almost all his chess-playing life in England. His tournament successes, which included firsts at Hamburg, 1885, and London, 1888, secured his recognition as a contender for Steinitz's world title. Unsuccessful in this, he concentrated on chess journalism and practically retired from serious play.

FRENCH DEFENSE

White	Black
Tarrasch	Gunsberg

1.	P—K4	P—K3
2.	P—Q4	P—Q4
3.	N—QB3	P×P
4.	N×P	N—KB3
5.	B—Q3	QN—Q2
6.	B—K3	N×N
7.	B×N	N—B3
8.	B—Q3	B—Q2

In this rather cramped variation, the best spot for the Queen Bishop is QN2. Black is therefore better advised to play 8 . . . , B—K2; 9 N—B3, P—QN3, etc.

9. **N—B3**	**B—Q3**
10. **O—O**	**N—N5?**
11. **B—KN5**	**P—KB3?**

Black's previous move was waste of time; this one is weakening. He has nothing better than 11 . . . , B—K2.

12. **B—Q2**	**Q—K2**
13. **P—KR3**	**N—R3**
14. **P—B4**	**P—B3**
15. **P—QN4!**	

Now White is in position to attack no matter how Black castles, for 15 . . . , O—O is answered by 16 B×N, etc.

So Black must castle into trouble, for he cannot play 15 . . . , B×P, to which Tarrasch gives the answer as 16 B×B, Q×B; 17 R—N1, Q—Q3; 18 R×P, O—O; 19 Q—B2, P—KB4; 20 P—B5, Q—Q4; 21 B—B4, Q—K5; 22 Q—B1, B—B1; 23 R—QB7, P—B5; 24 R—K1, Q—N3; 25 R×B, QR×R; 26 R×P, winning. A long but convincing analysis.

15.	**O—O—O**
16. **R—K1!?**	

Tarrasch later recommended 16 P—B5, followed by P—QR4 and P—N5, as much simpler.

16.	**B×P**
17. **R—N1**	**B×B**
18. **Q×B**	**K—N1**

So as to defend the Queen Knight Pawn with the Bishop, the threat otherwise being 19 Q—N2, B—K1; 20 R×P.

19. **P—B5**	**B—B1**
20. **R—N3**	**Q—QB2**
21. **KR—N1**	**K—R1**
22. **R—N6!**	

The attack now becomes fierce and brilliant. If now 22 . . . , P×R; 23 P×P, Q—Q3; 24 Q—R5ch., followed by mate.

22.	**P—K4**
23. **R/N1—N4!**	**KR—K1**

Beginning counteraction in the center just in time; the threat is . . . , P—K5, and it now becomes a race between White's attempts to break through on the wing and Black's to break through in the center.

23 . . . , P×R? is still fatal because of 24 BP×P, Q—Q3; 25 R—R4ch., K—N1; 26 R—R8ch.! K×R; 27 Q—R5ch., etc.

24. **P×P**	**P×P**
25. **R—QR4**	**P—K5**
26. **Q—R5**	**Q—N1**
27. **B×P**	**B—B4?**

The culmination of Black's counterplay: all his pieces come to life, and White cannot move the Bishop because of 28 . . . , R—Q8ch.; 29 N—K1, R/Q8×Nch.

Nevertheless, 27 . . . , R—Q8ch.; 28 N—K1, N—B4, is preferable.

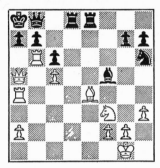

28. R—R6!!

Attack and counterattack continue in delicate balance. Now White threatens mate in two, and if 28 . . . , P×R; 29 B×Pch., etc.

28.	R—Q8ch.

All of Black's remaining moves are practically forced!

29. N—K1	R×Nch.

Apparently turning the tide in his favor, but White is not finished yet.

30. Q×R	B×B
31. R×B!	

The saving clause. 31 R×Pch., Q×R; 32 R×Qch., K×R; 33 P—B3, B—N3; 34 Q—R5ch., leaves him very problematical drawing chances. The text move gives up a piece but wins the game.

31.	R×R
32. Q×R	P×R
33. Q×Pch.	Q—QN2
34. Q—K8ch.	Q—N1
35. Q—K4ch.	Q—N2
36. P—B6!	

The key to his 28th move.

36.	Q—QB2
37. Q—K8ch.	Q—N1
38. Q—Q7!	Q—N8ch.

There is no longer any defense to the threat of P—B7.

39. K—R2	N—B4
40. P—B7	Resigns

GAME 12

Weiss—Tchigorin

NEW YORK, 1889

(Tie-Match for First Prize)

Max Weiss (1857–1927), during the few years in which he participated in master chess, was a frequent prize winner. His biggest success was in his last tournament, when he tied for first prize at New York, 1889. He was a Hungarian.

Michael I. Tchigorin (1850–1908) was the greatest Russian master of the second half of the nineteenth century. His aggressive unorthodoxy secured him many prizes, of which his tie for first prize at New York, 1889, was one of the most noteworthy. He unsuccessfully contested two matches with Steinitz for the world title.

RUY LOPEZ

	White	Black
	Weiss	Tchigorin
1.	P–K4	P–K4
2.	N–KB3	N–QB3
3.	B–N5	P–QR3
4.	B–R4	N–B3
5.	N–B3	B–N5

Questionable, as White's reply indicates.

| 6. | N–Q5 | B–K2 |

If 6 . . . , N×P?; 7 B×N wins a piece.

7.	P–Q3	P–Q3
8.	N×B	Q×N
9.	P–B3	P–R3
10.	P–KR3	O–O!?

The combination of Black's last two moves shows that he has no respect for his opponent's intended Pawn-storming attack.

11. P–KN4

The only practical consequence of this threatening gesture is that White's KB4 becomes weak and subject later on to Tchigorin's clever exploitation.

| 11. | | N–KR2 |

To prevent 12 P–N5, and also to prepare for the eventual . . . , P–KN4.

12.	KR–N1	N–Q1!
13.	B–K3	N–K3!
14.	P–R4	P–KN4!
15.	P×P	

Weiss hopes to make something of the open King Rook file, but his courage is more laudable than his judgment.

| 15. | | P×P |
| 16. | Q–K2 | Q–B3! |

He prevents White from playing 17 Q–B1 and 18 Q–

48

R3, and also prepares to occupy KB5.

17.	O–O–O	N–B5
18.	B×N	Q×Bch.
19.	N–Q2	

Forced, as he cannot permit . . . , B×P.

Black has now managed to obtain a clear initiative, and in what appears to be a solid position he soon produces a series of tactical threats in order to reinforce and increase his advantage.

19.	K–N2

Preparing to fight for the open file.

20.	P–B3	B–K3
21.	B–N3	R–R1
22.	R–R1	N–B3
23.	K–N1	B–Q2!

This threatens 24 . . . , N× NP!; 25 P×N, B×P; 26 Q–N2, B×R—which cannot be played at once, as 23 . . . , N×NP? is refuted by 24 B×B!

24.	R/Q1–N1	P–N4!
25.	N–B1	P–R4!

The Queen-side play seems to be irrelevant to the struggle for the King Rook file, but only in appearance. The connection will become clear three moves later.

26. P–R3

Hoping to prevent . . . , P–N5; actually, he increases its force!

26.	P–N5!

A deep sacrifice with a subtle point that was overlooked by the great Steinitz in his annotations.

27.	BP×P	P×P

28. R×R

He must renounce the open file in order to put an end to Black's Queen-side threat.

Steinitz recommended 28 P×P?? overlooking 28 . . . , R–R8ch.!!; 29 K×R, Q–B8ch.; 30 K–R2, R–R1ch.; 31 B–R4, B–K3ch.; 32 P–N3, R×B mate!

With the loss of the King Rook file, White's position is seen to be exceedingly precarious, as numerous possibilities of penetration present themselves to Black.

28.		R×R
29.	P×P	R–R6
30.	B–Q1	

White's extra Pawn is negligible indeed in comparison to the pressure exerted by Black's Rook and the purely defensive function of the White Bishop engaged in guarding White's feeble Pawn cluster.

50   WEISS—TCHIGORIN

| 30. | B—N4! |
| 31. N—K3 | K—B1 |

Eliminating a possible N—B5ch. and thereby threatening 32 . . . , N×KP!; 33 BP×N, R×N.

| 32. N—B4 | R—R7?! |

Although this move looks very strong, it is quite inferior to the winning line later proposed by Tchigorin: 32 . . . , P—Q4!; 33 P×P, N×QP; 34 N—R3 (34 Q×P? loses a piece by 34 . . . , B×N!; 35 Q×Q, B×Pch.), R—R7; 35 Q—B1, Q—Q7; 36 B—B2, N×P, and White can resign.

33. R—N2	R—R8
34. K—B2	P—Q4!
35. N—R3!	

If 35 P×P, N×QP, and Black's Knight has become too powerful:

a) 36 Q×P??, Q×Q; 37 N×Q, N—K6ch., winning the Rook.

b) 36 K—N3, B×Nch.; 37 P×B, N—K6; with a quick win for Black.

| 35. | B—B3 |
| 36. P—N5 | B—N2 |

The threat is now 37 . . . , P×P; 38 QP×P, N×KP!; 39 P×N, Q×Pch., winning the Rook.

| 37. R—B2 | R—N8! |

Setting the stage for a further inroad that is not without its dangers. White must not play 38 R—N2? be-

cause of 38 . . . , R×R; 39 Q×R, P×P; 40 QP×P, N×KP!

38. Q—Q2!

He sees through Black's plan and undertakes cold-blooded countermeasures.

38.	Q—N6!?
39. R—R2!	P×P
40. QP×P	

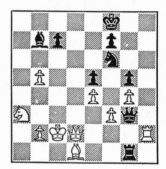

Now we see how risky Tchigorin's winning attempt is. White is threatening to win with 41 Q—Q8ch.

40.   R×B!!

So that if 41 K×R (obviously 41 Q×R?? will not do), Q×Pch. with these possibilities:

a) 42 K—B1, Q—B8ch.; 43 Q—Q1, Q—KB5ch.; 44 R—Q2, N×KP, with a winning game.

b) 42 R—K2, B×P; 43 Q—Q8ch., K—N2; 44 Q×P, N×P, with a dangerous attack.

41. R—R8ch.!!

A magnificent counterattack that comes within an ace of

winning. So White gets some use out of the open file after all!

41.		K—N2
42.	Q×Pch.!	K×R
43.	Q×Nch.	K—N1
44.	K×R	Q—B7!

Now it is Black who must fight for a draw, as he comes out a Pawn down.

45. N—B2?

Steinitz considers that White has a slow but certain win with 45 K—B1, Q—B8ch.; 46 K—Q2, Q—B7ch.; 47 K—B3, Q—Q5ch.; 48 K—B2, B—B1; 49 Q—N5ch., and 50 Q—Q2.

45.		Q—B8ch.
46.	K—Q2	Q×NP

47.	P—N4	B—R3
48.	Q—Q8ch.	K—R2
49.	Q×P	Q—Q6ch.
50.	K—B1	Q×BP

Black is obviously much better off than in the previous note.

51.	Q×P	Q×NP
52.	Q—B5ch.	Q×Q
53.	P×Q	K—N2

Even with the Queens off, White cannot win.

54.	K—Q2	K—B3
55.	N—Q4	K—K4
56.	K—B3	P—B3
	Drawn	

For if 57 P—N5, B×P, etc. A great game up to the very last situation.

GAME 13

Taubenhaus—Tarrasch

NUREMBERG, 1892

Jean Taubenhaus (1850–1919) was born in Poland but spent most of his life in Paris. His chief success was a match victory against Albin.

EVANS GAMBIT

White	*Black*
Taubenhaus	Tarrasch
1. P—K4	P—K4
2. N—KB3	N—QB3
3. B—B4	B—B4
4. P—QN4	B×P
5. P—B3	B—R4

6. P—Q4	P×P
7. O—O	P×P

The famous "Compromised Defense," with which Black sets himself a trying defensive task in return for two temporarily worthless Pawns.

| 8. Q–N3 | Q–B3 |
| 9. P–K5 | Q–N3 |

9 . . . , N×P? loses a piece (10 R–K1, P–Q3; 11 Q–R4ch.).

| 10. N×P | KN–K2 |
| 11. N–K2 | |

The book move is 11 B–R3! making Black's life very hard indeed.

| 11. | P–N4! |

Offering back one of the Pawns in order to deprive White's attack of some momentum. For precisely this reason, White spurns the Pawn.

12. B–Q3	Q–K3
13. Q–N2	N–N3
14. N–B4	N×N
15. B×N	P–KR3
16. KR–Q1	P–R3
17. QR–B1	B–N2

Black's game remains uncomfortable. He hits on the rather novel idea of castling Queen-side.

18. B–K4	B–N3
19. N–R4	O–O–O!?
20. P–R4?	

Premature.

[See diagram in next column.]

| 20. | P×P? |

Missing his chance. Tarrasch gives this long but satisfying analysis to show

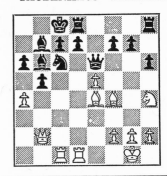

that Black has better: 20 . . . , P–N4!; 21 P×P, P×P; 22 B–B5, Q–K2; 23 Q×P, P×B; 24 R×N, B×R; 25 Q×QB, K–N1; 26 Q–R4, Q×N; 27 R–R1, Q×Pch.; 28 K–R1, P–B3, and White has shot his bolt.

21. B–Q5	Q–N5
22. B–KN3	P–N4
23. N–B3	KR–B1
24. R–B4	Q–B4
25. KR–QB1	P–B3!?

In a difficult situation, Black plays for more complications!

| 26. B–K4 | Q–K3 |
| 27. P×P! | Q×P! |

Better than 27 . . . , P–Q4; 28 B–B5!, Q×B; 29 R×N!, B×R; 30 R×B, with the troublesome threat of 31 Q×B. (If 30 . . . , K–N2; 31 R×Pch.!).

| 28. N–K5! | P–R6! |

A masterly resource. If 28 . . . , N×N?; 29 R×Pch.!, B×R; 30 Q×B mate.

Or 29 . . . , K—N1; 30 R× Bch., K—R1; 31 R×Bch., winning.

| 29. | Q—B2! | P—Q4! |
| 30. | R×N | B×R |

The crisis.

31. N×B?

This plausible move loses, as Tarrasch's superb play will demonstrate.

Correct, as Tarrasch later indicated, was 31 B—B5ch.!, Q×B; 32 Q×B, K—N1!; 33 N—Q7ch.!, K—R2!; 34 N×B, P×N; 35 Q—B7ch., K—R1; 36 Q—B6ch., etc., with a draw by perpetual check. A beautiful line of play!

31.		P×B
32.	N×R	Q×N
33.	Q—B6	Q—Q7
34.	Q—K6ch.	K—N2
35.	Q×Pch.	K—R2
36.	Q—QB4	R—Q1!

He spurns 36 . . . , B×Pch. The attack is definitely beaten back and the reaction has set in.

| 37. | P—R3 | Q—Q6! |

The exchange of Queens is now forced because of the neat variation 38 Q—KN4, R—Q5; 39 Q—B8, Q×B!; 40 P×Q, R—Q1ch., winning!

| 38. | Q×Q | R×Q |
| 39. | K—B1 | |

No better is 39 B×P, B—Q5!, etc.

39.		B—Q5
40.	R×Pch.	K—N3
41.	R—B2	B—N7
42.	K—K2	R—N6
	Resigns	

A very absorbing game from start to finish.

Pillsbury—Tarrasch

HASTINGS, 1895

Harry N. Pillsbury (1872–1906), an American player, was one of the greatest masters of his time, and his premature death was a tragic loss. He sprang to fame by winning the Hastings tournament (1895), ahead of almost all the world's great masters. His chess was marked by the will to win on almost all possible occasions.

QUEEN'S GAMBIT

DECLINED

White	Black
Pillsbury	Tarrasch
1. P–Q4	P–Q4
2. P–QB4	P–K3
3. N–QB3	N–KB3
4. B–N5	B–K2
5. N–B3	QN–Q2
6. R–B1	O–O
7. P–K3	P–QN3

In later years, this defense was to be superseded by 7 . . . , P–B3.

8. PXP	PXP
9. B–Q3	B–N2
10. O–O	P–B4

Both players are on familiar ground, Pillsbury playing the variation named after him, and Tarrasch striving for a Queen-side majority of Pawns, the advantage of which he took over from Steinitz's theories.

11. R–K1

The subsequent course of the game suggests that this is loss of time.

11.	P–B5
12. B–N1	P–QR3
13. N–K5!	P–N4
14. P–B4	R–K1
15. Q–B3	N–B1
16. N–K2!	

With a view to N–N3–B5 Black must simplify in order to relieve his cramped position.

| 16. | N–K5 |
| 17. BXB | RXB |

With a view to doubling Rooks on the King file later on.

18. BXN!

A rather surprising move since it gives Black more freedom, but in return he secures the free use of his KN3 and blocks any frontal attack on his weak King Pawn.

| 18. | P×B |
| 19. Q—N3! | P—B3 |

Safe enough now that White's King Bishop is gone, and at the same time both driving White from his outpost and forestalling any attack by P—B5—B6.

20. N—N4	K—R1
21. P—B5!	Q—Q2
22. R—B1!	R—Q1

Black loses time here and later. He should guard the artificially isolated King Pawn and proceed with the advance of the Queen-side Pawns.

| 23. R—B4 | Q—Q3 |
| 24. Q—R4! | QR—K1 |

25. N—B3?

Serious loss of time in a critical situation. Correct is 25 N—B2, B—Q4; 26 P—KN4!, P—R3!; 27 Q—N3, P—N5; 28 P—KR4, etc. Now the advantage shifts to Black.

| 25. | Q—B3 |
| 26. N—B2 | B—Q4 |

| 27. R—B1 | P—N5 |
| 28. N—K2 | |

The drama begins to develop. White's Queen side seems defenseless.

| 28. | Q—R5 |
| 29. N—N4! | |

So that if 29 . . . , Q×P?; 30 N×P!, P×N; 31 Q×BPch., and wins.

| 29. | N—Q2 |
| 30. R/B4—B2! | |

And now 30 . . . , Q×P loses because of 31 N—B4, B—B2; 32 N—N6ch., B×N; 33 P×B:

a) 33 . . . , P—R3; 34 N× RP!! (threatens mate in two), P×N; 35 Q×RPch., K—N1; 36 R—B5! and 37 R—R5.

b) 33 . . . , N—B1; 34 N× P!, P×N; 35 R×P, K—N1; 36 R—B7, and wins.

| 30. | K—N1 |
| 31. N—B1 | P—B6! |

Now it is Black's turn again, and he forces a dangerous passed Pawn.

32. P—QN3!	Q—B3
33. P—KR3	P—QR4
34. N—R2	P—R5
35. P—N4	P×P
36. P×P	R—R1?

This game was played in the second round, Pillsbury having lost a magnificent game in the first round to Tchigorin. Had Tarrasch known that his opponent was more than a mere outsider, he would have paid his respects to White's

attack by stopping for 36 . . . ,
P—R3! and if 37 Q—N3, N—
B1!; 38 P—R4, N—R2! when
White's attack is much slower
than in the text continuation.

37. **P—N5!**   **R—R6**
38. **N—N4!**

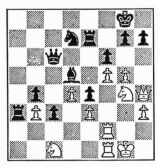

38.   **B×P**

Even the preservation of
this Bishop does not help: 38
. . . , R×P; 39 N×R, B×N; 40
R—KN2, K—R1; 41 P×P, P×P;
42 N—K5!, N×N; 43 P×N, P—
B7 (if 43 . . . , R×P; 44 Q—R6!
decides); 44 P—K6! and wins.

39. **R—KN2!**

A threat again at last,
though it seems to have come
almost too late. The intention
is 40 P×P, when Black cannot
recapture.

Note that the text move
gains a priceless tempo as
against 39 N×B?, R×N; 40
R—KN2, R—N7!

39.   **K—R1**

No better is 39 . . . , P×P;
40 Q×P, K—B1; 41 N×B, R×
N; 42 P—B6, etc.

40. **P×P**   **P×P**

Or 40 . . . , N×P; 41 N—K5,
Q—K1; 42 N—N6ch., etc.

41. **N×B!**

The key to his plan. Black's
Rook is out of the game at
QN6, and his KN1 is sadly in
need of protection.

41.   **R×N**
42. **N—R6!**   **R—N2**

The only answer to the
threat of 43 R—N8 mate; for
if 42 . . . , R—K1?; 43 N—B7
mate!

43. **R×R**   **K×R**
44. **Q—N3ch.!!**   **K×N**

If 44 . . . , K—B1; 45 Q—
N8ch., picking up the unfortunate Rook at QN6!

45. **K—R1!!**

The final point of Pillsbury's
exquisite timing. 45 R—B4
allows Black to draw with 45
. . . , R—N8ch., etc.

45.   **Q—Q4**

White was threatening 46
R—KN1 and 47 Q—R4 mate.

46. **R—KN1**   **Q×BP**
47. **Q—R4ch.**   **Q—R4**
48. **Q—B4ch.**   **Q—N4**
49. **R×Q**   **P×R**
50. **Q—Q6ch.**   **K—R4**
51. **Q×N**   **P—B7**
52. **Q×P** mate

This famous game, which
acquainted the chess world
with one of its greatest gen-
iuses, gave 1 P—Q4 a vogue
which persists to this very
day.

GAME 15

Steinitz–Pillsbury

ST. PETERSBURG, 1896

PETROFF DEFENSE

White	Black
Steinitz	Pillsbury
1. P–K4	P–K4
2. N–KB3	N–KB3
3. P–Q4	

Steinitz's own method of treating the Petroff Defense, introduced into master play for the first time in this game.

3.	PxP
4. P–K5	N–K5
5. Q–K2	

More usual, and certainly less adventurous, is 5 QxP, P–Q4; 6 PxP e.p., NxQP; 7 B–N5, etc.

| 5. | B–N5ch.!? |

Hoping to be able to exchange his Knight on his Q7, White being unable to play 6 P–B3? because of 6 . . . , PxP; 7 QxN, PxPch.; 8 QxB, PxB(Q)ch.

6. K–Q1!?	P–Q4
7. PxP e.p.	P–KB4
8. N–N5!?	

Though this wins a piece by the threats of Q–B4 and P–KB3, Steinitz had previously condemned it as a "seductive" move leading to a lost game!

8.	O–O!
9. Q–B4ch.	K–R1

10. QxB!

A new discovery, previously not considered because of the answer . . . , NxPch. The more obvious alternatives to the text fail, for example:

a) 10 PxP, NxPch.; 11 K–K2, Q–K2ch.; 12 KxN, Q–K8ch.; 13 K–B3, QxB threatening . . . , Q–K6 mate.

b) 10 NxN, PxN; 11 QxB, N–B3; 12 Q–Q2, B–N5ch.; 13 B–K2, RxP; 14 R–K1, Q–B3; 15 P–B3, RxB; 16 RxR, Q–B8ch. and wins.

10.	N–QB3
11. Q–R3!	

After 11 Q–K1, NxN; 12 PxP, Q–B3; 13 BxN, QxB, Black has the better game.

Steinitz avoids this line by his veiled attack on the Black Rook. Black must therefore accept the offer of the exchange as his best chance, and the game becomes intensely exciting.

11.	N×Pch.
12.	K—K1	N×R
13.	P×P	Q—K1ch.
14.	B—K2	P—B5!

Seriously cramping White's position. Should White reply 15 P—R3 (to prevent . . . , B—N5 or an eventual . . . , N—N5), the cornered Knight gets out by . . . , N—N6.

| 15. | K—B1 | B—Q2 |
| 16. | N—Q2 | N—K4! |

Another attempt to extricate his Knight by 17 . . . , N—N5 and if 18 B×N, B—N4ch.

White's position is one that calls for all the famed defensive skill of Steinitz. He is the exchange down, the imprisoned Knight is destined to escape, and Black's pressure continues to be harassing. The way in which Steinitz resourcefully combines attack with defense is quite fascinating. Even the apparently idle Pawn at QB7 is soon impressed into service!

17. N/Q2—B3!

Not 17 K—N1, N—N5; 18 Q—KB3 (if 18 B×N, Q—K8ch., and mate follows, or

18 K×N, Q×B, etc.), Q—K6ch.:

a) 19 Q×Q, BP×Q; 20 K× N, P×N, with advantage to Black.

b) 19 K×N??, N—B7ch.; 20 K—N1, N—R6ch.; 21 K—B1, Q—N8 mate.

| 17. | N—N5 |
| 18. | B—Q3! |

White has been forced to submit to the escape of the Knight, so he prepares a counterattack.

18.   N/R8—B7

Plausible, but 18 . . . , P—KR3 is best.

19. B×RP!   B—N4ch.

Underestimating White's resources and hoping to force the issue by his own attack.

Correct is 19 . . . , N—B3; 20 B—B5, N/B7—N5. After Black misses this chance, White arduously establishes his superiority.

20. K—N1   Q—K7

Threatening . . . , Q—B8 mate.

21. B—Q2   N—Q8

Not quite sufficient is 21 . . . , N—K6 (threatening to mate by . . . , N—R6ch., etc.), because of 22 N—R4! defending the threatened mate and also threatening 23 N—N6 mate!

White is suddenly seen to have no small counterattack!

The text move, however, again threatens . . . , Q—B8 mate, and the fact that both players have mating threats at their disposal is an indication of the critical nature of the position.

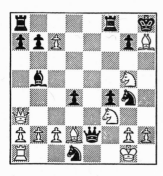

22. **B—Q3!**

This contains the attack, as the following variations show: 22 . . . , Q—B7ch.; 23 K—R1, N/Q8—K6; 24 B×N, N×B; 25 R—KN1, B—B3; 26 Q—Q6, R—B3; 27 N—B7ch.! and now:

a) 27 . . . , R×N; 28 Q—N6, K—N1; 29 Q—R7ch., K—B1; 30 Q—R8ch., K—K2; 31 Q×R, B×N; 32 Q—Q8ch., K—K3; 33 P—B8(Q)ch., and wins.

b) 27 . . . , K—N1; 28 Q—Q8ch., R×Q; 29 P×R(Q)ch., K×N; 30 N—N5 mate.

22.		B×B
23.	Q×B	Q×Q
24.	P×Q	N×NP

This allows White to bring his Rook to the support of his passed Pawn, but if 24 . . . , N/Q8—K6; 25 N—K6 obtain-

ing at least material equality and a positional advantage.

25.	R—N1	N×QP
26.	R×P	N—B4
27.	R—N5	N—QR3
28.	N—K6	R—B3

The battle continues unabated. If 28 . . . , KR—B1; 29 R—R5ch., K—N1; 30 R—KN5, N—K6; 31 R×Pch., with an easy win.

29. **N/B3×P   R—K1**

. . . , R—QB1 saves a useful tempo, without offering Black any real hope. The text move prepares a trap that Steinitz sees through without any difficulty.

30.	R—R5ch.	K—N1
31.	R—KN5	

But not 31 B×P?, R×B; 32 N×R, R—K8 mate.

31.		N—K6
32.	N×NP	R—QB1
33.	N—K6ch.	K—R1

If 33 . . . , K—B2; 34 R—N7ch., K—K1; 35 R—N8ch., K—Q2; 36 R—Q8ch., and Black can resign.

But the position of Black's King on the edge of the board allows White to develop sharp attacking threats.

34.	B—R5	R—B2
35.	N—K2	R—B4

White was threatening 36 B—B3ch., K—R2; 37 R—R5ch., K—N3; 38 N/K2×Pch., R×N; 39 N×Rch., K—B2; 40 R—R7ch., winning.

36.	B—B3ch.	K—R2
37.	R—N7ch.	K—R3
38.	N/K2×P	N×BP

Getting rid of the objectionable Pawn at last, for if now 39 R×N, R×R; 40 N×R, R× N, and wins because of the threats of . . . , R—B8 mate and . . . , R—B5.

White, however, has a line to recover the exchange with a won ending.

39.	R—N6ch.	K—R2
40.	N—N5ch.	R×N
41.	R×R	N—K1
42.	B—Q4	N—Q8
43.	R—R5ch.	K—N1
44.	R—R8ch.	K—B2
45.	R—R7ch.	K—N1
46.	R—K7	R—Q1
47.	N—K6	R—B1

| 48. | P—KR4 | N—B6 |
| 49. | B×N | |

There is no need for further complications. The struggle, one of exceptional ferocity, is now over.

49.		R×B
50.	R×Nch.	K—B2
51.	R—QR8	K×N
52.	R×P	K—B4
53.	R—R4	R—B7
54.	K—R2	R—Q7
55.	K—R3	R—Q6ch.
56.	P—N3	R—QB6
57.	R—R5ch.	K—N3
58.	P—R4	R—B5
59.	R—R6ch.	K—R4
60.	P—N4ch.	Resigns

For after 60 . . . , R×P there follows 61 R—R5ch.

GAME 16

Pillsbury—Tchigorin

ST. PETERSBURG, 1896

QUEEN'S GAMBIT
DECLINED

	White	Black
	Pillsbury	Tchigorin
1.	P—Q4	P—Q4
2.	P—QB4	N—QB3

Tchigorin's famous defense, which has not been regarded with great favor.

| 3. | N—KB3 | B—N5 |
| 4. | P—K3 | |

The modern move, which gives White the initiative, is 4 Q—R4.

4.		P—K3
5.	N—B3	B—N5
6.	Q—N3	B×N
7.	P×B	KN—K2

8. **B–Q2**   **O–O**
9. **P–B4**

If Black is allowed to play . . . , P–K4, he will have a very good game. After the text move, he has to have recourse to a most eccentric development if he is to get any counterplay.

9.   **R–N1!**
10. **O–O–O!?**

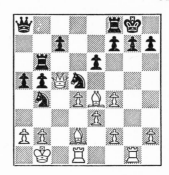

This risky move, all the more daring against a great master of attacking play, is typical of Pillsbury's enterprising style.

10.   **P×P**
11. **B×P**   **P–QN4!**
12. **B–Q3**

Not 12 B×NP?, B×N; 13 B×B, P–QR3, nor 12 N×P?, B×Bch.; 13 R×B, P–QR3, and White loses a piece either way.

12.   **B×N**
13. **Q×B**   **R–N3**

In order to play . . . , N–Q4. He also makes room for the Queen and toys with the possibility of . . . , N–K4. Hence White's reply.

14. **K–N1**   **P–QR4**
15. **KR–N1**   **N–N5**

He is not afraid of 16 P–Q5?, which loses material after 16 . . . , P–KB3.

16. **B–K4**   **N/K2–Q4**
17. **Q–B5**   **Q–R1!**

Black's whole scheme of development is strikingly irregular, yet White has to treat it with the utmost respect. The threat now is . . . , N–B6ch. followed by . . . , Q×Bch. with a well-posted Queen and a considerable reduction in White's attacking chances. But at the cost of exchanging pieces, White can now win a Pawn.

18. **QB×N**   **P×B**
19. **B×N**   **P×B**
20. **Q×P/N4**

Not 20 Q×BP?, R–QR3!

20.   **R–QR3**
21. **Q–N3**

The open Queen Rook file is good compensation to Black for his Pawn. White dare not open the Queen Knight file as well by 21 Q×P? because of 21 . . . , R–N1; 22 Q–K2, R×P.

Equally 21 P–QR3 allows Black to open the Queen Knight file by 21 . . . , R–R5; 22 Q–Q2, P–N5.

21.   R—N1
22. R—N5!

Owing to the weakness of Black's Queen Pawn, White is able to develop a counter-attack along his own open file without loss of time.

22.   P—QB3
23. QR—N1   P—N3
24. P—B5!   P—N5!
25. PxP   RPxP

It is now a critical race between the two attacks. Black threatens . . . , R—R6! but must first attend to his King side.

26. Q—Q3!

White has emerged with the initiative. If Black replies 26 . ▲ . . , RxP, then White breaks through with 27 Rx Pch., K—B1; 28 R—N8ch., transposing into the actual game.

26.   K—B1!

27. RxNP!   RxP!!

He dare not play 27 . . . , PxR? because of 28 QxP:

a) 28 . . . , RxP; 29 Q—B6ch., K—K1; 30 R—N8ch., K—Q2; 31 R—N7ch. and mate next move.

b) 28 . . . , R—R2; 29 Q—N8ch., K—K2; 30 Q—R7ch., K—K3; 31 Q—R6ch., K—Q2 (if 31 . . . , K—B4; 32 Q—N6 mate); 32 R—N7ch. and mate next move.

28. R—N8ch.   K—K2
29. RxR   Q—R5!

Black now seems to be in great trouble, having lost a whole Rook. He has, however, this fighting reply, which by its threat of . . . , R—R8 mate ensures recovery of the piece.

30. R—N7ch.   K—K3
31. K—B1!

He has nothing better, for if he tries to return the Rook in what seems to be a more advantageous manner by 31 R—N6ch.?, P—B3; 32 RxPch., KxR; 33 K—B1, Black still has a mate: 33 . . . , R—R8ch.; 34 K—Q2, Q—Q8 mate.

31.   R—R8ch.
32. K—Q2   RxR
33. Q—B2

If 33 Q—K2, Q—R8, threatening both . . . , QxPch. and . . . , Q—B8ch.
Black will now recover the Pawn with a drawn ending. The fireworks are over.

33.   QxQch.
34. KxQ   R—N7
35. RxNP   RxP
36. R—N7   RxPch.

37. K–Q3   P–KB4

The game could be abandoned as a draw.

38.	R–QB7	K–Q3
39.	R–B7	P–B4
40.	PXPch.	KXP
41.	R–B7ch.	K–Q3
42.	R–B2	R–B6
43.	K–Q4	R–R6
44.	R–B2	K–K3
45.	P–N4	R–R5ch.
46.	R–B4	R–R8
47.	K–B5	R–B8ch.
48.	K–Q4	

Not 48 K–N6, R–B6.

48.		R–QN8
49.	K–B3	R–K8
50.	K–Q2	R–QR8
51.	K–Q3	R–R6ch.
52.	K–K2	K–K4
53.	R–Q4	R–N6
54.	R–KB4	R–B6
55.	K–Q2	R–B1
56.	K–Q3	R–B8
57.	K–Q2	R–QR8
58.	K–K2	R–R7ch.
59.	K–Q3	R–KN7
60.	K–B3	R–K7
61.	K–Q3	R–QR7
62.	K–B3	Drawn

GAME 17

Charousek–Pillsbury

NUREMBERG, 1896

Rudolf Charousek (1873–99) was a Czech by birth but Hungarian by adoption. In a very brief career before he was overtaken by tuberculosis, he showed himself a player of the very first rank, his most striking achievement being the winning of the Berlin, 1897, tournament.

FALKBEER COUNTER
GAMBIT

	White	Black
	Charousek	Pillsbury
1.	P–K4	P–K4
2.	P–KB4	P–Q4
3.	KPXP	P–K5
4.	P–Q3	N–KB3
5.	PXP	

In later years 5 N–Q2 (strongly recommended by Keres) has had a considerable vogue.

| 5. | | NXKP |
| 6. | Q–K2!? | |

The usual line is 6 N–KB3, B–QB4; 7 Q–K2, B–B4. But Charousek is leading to a new variation of his own on the 8th move.

6.	Q×P
7. N—Q2	P—KB4
8. P—KN4!?	B—K2

Pillsbury later concluded that 8 . . . , N—B3 is best.

9. B—N2	Q—R4
10. P×P	

10 B×N? wins a Pawn but cedes Black a tremendous initiative.

10.	N—KB3

10 . . . , N—Q3 has points, as later on Black can play . . . , B—B3 as well as . . . , N×P.

11. N—B3	O—O
12. O—O	Q—B4ch.?

An indifferent method of defending the Bishop. 12 . . . , N—B3 is preferable.

13. K—R1	N—B3
14. N—N3	Q×KBP
15. KN—Q4	N×N
16. N×N	Q—B4

Had he omitted 12 . . . , Q—B4ch., he could now play 16 . . . , B—B4 pinning the Knight.

17. N—K6!	B×N
18. Q×Bch.	K—R1
19. B—K3	

In this open position, White's Bishops are very strong, and his marked initiative soon gives him formidable attacking prospects.

19.	Q—Q3
20. Q—N3	P—B3

21. QR—Q1	Q—B2
22. B—Q2!	

The posting of this Bishop on the long diagonal will subject Black to serious threats.

22.	QR—K1?

Apparently Pillsbury does not realize the dangers lurking in the position. He should seek safety in 22 . . . , QR—Q1!; 23 Q—N3, N—Q4; 24 B×N, R×B; 25 B—B3, B—B3!

23. Q—N3	B—Q3
24. B—QB3	R—K2
25. Q—R4	N—Q4?!

Leading to situations of critical intensity in which he hopes to outmaneuver his opponent.

26. B×N	P×B
27. Q—R5	B×P

28. Q×P!

28 B—N4 is answered by 28 . . . , R—K4!:
 a) 29 Q—N4, Q×P (not 29 . . . , R—N4?; 30 Q×R!); 30 Q—R3 (if 30 R×B, R×R; 31 Q×R, Q×Rch.), Q—K5ch. etc.

b) 29 Q–R4, P–KN4; 30 Q–R3, R–K6; 31 Q–R5, R/ B1–K1.

After the text move, though there are no absolutely immediate threats, Black finds that his ingenuity may recoil on himself, for danger is imminent owing to the pin on his Bishop, to the pressure on the long diagonal, and to the possibility in some eventualities of mate on the first rank.

| 28. | **R–KN1** |
| 29. **R–Q4!** | **B–K4!?** |

Not 29 . . . , B×P?; 30 R–KR4!, B–N6; 31 R×Pch.!, K× R; 32 Q–R5 mate.

30. R–QB4!

Preventing the exchange of Bishops and prepared to answer 30 . . . , Q–Q3? with 31 Q×Rch.! forcing mate.

| *30.* | **Q–N1** |
| *31.* **R–K1!** | |

In this complicated situation, 31 R–K4!? looks conclusive, but Black has a way out:
   a) 31 . . . , B–Q3?; 32 R–KR4!, B–K4; 33 R×Pch.!, K× R; 34 Q–K4ch., K–R3; 35 Q–R4ch., winning.
   b) 31 . . . , R–KB1!; 32 R–Q1, B–Q3; 33 R–KR4, B–B5!, holding everything.

| *31.* | **R–Q1** |

White cannot play 32 B× B?, as Black simply replies 32 . . . , R×Q and the Bishop is pinned. But apparently Black's move is still insufficient.

32. Q–B5?!

For, as G. W. Baines pointed out, White can now play 32 R×B!, R×Q; 33 R×R/K7, and there is no satisfactory answer to the four threats of B×Pch., R×KNP, R/B4–B7, and R/ B4–K4.

His main analysis continues 33 . . . , R–Q8ch.; 34 K–N2, Q–Q1; 35 R/B4–K4, R– Q7ch.; 36 K–R3, Q–B1ch.; 37 K–N3, R–Q1; 38 R–KN4, R–N1; 39 B–K5, Q–B1 (if 39 . . . , Q×P; 40 B×Pch.! forces mate); 40 R/K7×KNP, with a won ending.

| 32. | **B–Q3!** |
| 33. **R×R!** | |

The right idea just too late!

| 33. | **B×Q** |
| 34. **R×KNP!** | |

If 34 R×B, Q–B5!; 35 R× KNP, R–Q5!

| 34. | **R–Q8ch.!** |
| 35. **R–N1ch.** | **B–Q5!** |

The complications of defense with counterattack on

both sides constitute chess of
the richest quality.

36.	B×Bch.	R×B
37.	R×R	Q–KB1!

Now the two Rooks are in-
sufficient to win against the
threat of perpetual check,
though Charousek still tries
hard to force the issue.

38.	R–Q3	Q–K2
39.	P–KR3	P–KR4

Forestalling any chance of
mate on his KN1. White's attempts to get a Rook onto the
King Rook file with check are
neatly foiled.

40.	R/Q3–KN3	Q–K5ch.
41.	R/N1–N2	Q–K8ch.
42.	K–R2	Q–K4
43.	P–KR4	Q–B5
44.	K–N1	Q×P
45.	P–B3	Q–KB5
46.	R–N5	Q–K6ch.
47.	K–R2	Q–B6
48.	R/N2–N3	Q–K7ch.
49.	K–R3	Q–K3ch.
50.	K–R4	Q–K5ch.
	Drawn	

For if 51 K×P, Q–R2ch.;
52 K–N4, Q–K5ch.; 53 K–R3,
Q–R8ch. "A game worthy of
the first meeting between two
of the finest players who ever
lived."—Sergeant.

GAME 18

Steinitz—Lasker

WORLD CHAMPIONSHIP MATCH, 1896

Dr. Emanuel Lasker (1868–1941) was world champion from 1894 to 1921, and through the whole of his playing career no master was ever more dangerous or more difficult to defeat. Yet he had no definable style; he sought even at the cost of some temporary disadvantage to create a position where his skill could be given full play. His philosophy of the struggle to succeed by any means was applied by him to the chessboard as to life. He achieved a wonderful succession of victories, among the greatest being his first prizes at St. Petersburg, 1896; Nuremberg, 1896; London, 1899; Paris, 1900; St. Petersburg, 1909; St. Petersburg, 1914; and New York, 1924—not to mention the successful matches against Steinitz, Marshall, Tarrasch, and Janowski.

QUEEN'S GAMBIT
DECLINED

	White	Black
	Steinitz	Lasker
1.	P–Q4	P–Q4
2.	P–QB4	P–K3
3.	N–QB3	N–KB3
4.	B–N5	B–K2
5.	P–K3	O–O
6.	Q–N3	

A favorite with Steinitz, but it has long since become obsolete.

6.		P×P
7.	B×P	P–B4
8.	P×P	Q–R4
9.	N–B3	Q×BP
10.	O–O	N–B3

Threatening to win a piece by . . . , N–QR4.

| 11. | B–Q3 | |

11 B–K2 looks more natural, but White plans an attack along the diagonal.

| 11. | | N–QN5 |
| 12. | B×N | P×B |

Black cannot avoid the breakup of his King-side Pawns.

If 12 . . . , B×B; 13 N–K4, Q–N3; 14 N×Bch., etc.

Or 12 . . . , N×B; 13 N–K4, Q–Q4; 14 Q×Q, P×Q; 15 B×B, R–K1; 16 N–B6ch., P×N; 17 B×P, winning a Pawn.

| 13. | B–N1 | |

The natural continuation after his 11th move, although it shuts in the Queen Rook.

13.		R–Q1
14.	P–QR3	N–Q4
15.	Q–B2	P–B4

16.	N–Q4	B–B3
17.	P–KN4!?	N×N

After White's last violent move, which also has obvious weaknesses, Black decides to play for a win. There is a clear draw by 17 . . . , B×N; 18 P× B, Q×QP; 19 P×P, Q–N5ch.; 20 K–R1, Q–B6ch., etc.

18.	P×N	P×P
19.	Q×Pch.	K–B1
20.	B–K4!	

For all the constricting appearance of his 13th move, his Queen Rook is free for action before Black's even now.

20.		K–K2

Threatening 21 . . . , R–R1 winning the Queen!

21.	B–N6!	R–B1
22.	QR–N1!	Q–KN4

Black hopes to turn the opening of the King side to his own ends.

23.	B–B2	R–R1
24.	Q–K4	

Now the sacrifice R×Pch. is in the air, and Black must make room for his King at KB3.

24.		B–K4
25.	KR–Q1	B×Pch.
26.	K–B1	

Now Black should continue 26 . . . , P–N3!, and if 27 N–B6ch. (not 27 Q×R??, B–

R3ch.), K–B1; 28 Q–N4ch., K–N2; 29 Q–Q4ch., P–K4; 30 Q–Q3, B–N2, with a Pawn up and the better position.

26.		P–B4?
27.	R×Pch.!	

Seizing the opportunity to reassume the initiative with a fine sacrificial attack against Black's exposed King.

27.		B×R!

As usual, Lasker defends with great coolness in an inordinately difficult situation. The acceptance of the sacrifice is his best chance, for example:

a) 27 . . . , K–B1? (or 27 . . . , K–K1?; 28 B–R4ch., etc.); 28 N×Pch., leading to mate.

b) 27 . . . , K–B3?; 28 Q–B6, Q–N1 (not 28 . . . , B× R?; 29 Q×Pch., K–N2; 30 N×Pch., K–B1; 31 R–Q7, forcing mate); 29 R–N5, and wins.

28.	Q×Bch.	K–B3

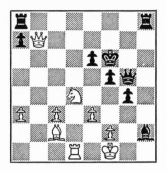

29. N×KP?!

And now White in turn misses the best move, which was 29 N×BP!, for example:

a) 29 . . . , P×N?; 30 Q–B6ch., K–B2; 31 R–Q7ch., and wins.

b) 29 . . . , Q–N1?; 30 Q–K7ch. and now A. 30 . . . , K–K4; 31 N–Q6!, R–QB1; 32 P–QB4!, R×P; 33 N×R mate, or B. 30 . . . , K–N3; 31 N–N7ch., K–R3; 32 Q–B6 mate.

c) 29 . . . , QR–K1; 30 R–Q7, with a winning attack.

29.   **Q–N1!**

Not 29 . . . , K×N?; 30 B–N3ch., K–K4; 31 Q–Q5ch., K–B3; 32 Q–B7ch., K–K4; 33 Q–K6 mate.

30. N–Q4!

White's attack dies away after 30 N–B5?, Q–B5ch.; 31 N–Q3, or 30 N–B7?, B×N.

He therefore plays for material compensation for his sacrifice.

30.   **R–Q1!**

In order to be able to answer 31 Q–B6ch. with 31 . . . , R–Q3.

31.	B×P	B–K4!
32.	B–K4	Q–B5ch.!
33.	B–Q3!	Q×P
34.	Q–K4	B×N
35.	P×B	

Preferring to have the King file open before taking the checks.

35.   **Q×QP**

36. Q–N6ch.

Now he has lost his material equality but again has sufficient positional compensation to secure the draw.

| 36. | K–K2 |
| 37. | R–K1ch. | K–B1 |

If 37 . . . , K–Q2, White draws by 38 Q–K6ch., K–B2; 39 R–B1ch., K–N1; 40 R–N1ch., K–B2; 41 R–B1ch., etc.

38.	Q–B5ch.	K–N1
39.	Q–N6ch.	K–B1
	Drawn	

A fair ending to a game which both players tried to win, and which was all the keener for the failure to find the best continuations at all times.

GAME 19

Lasker—Blackburne

LONDON, 1899

RUY LOPEZ

	White Lasker	Black Blackburne
1.	P–K4	P–K4
2.	N–KB3	N–QB3
3.	B–N5	P–Q3
4.	P–Q4	B–Q2
5.	P–Q5?!	

A most unusual move, which relieves the tension in the center but gives him a certain space advantage. His next move is the necessary corollary, otherwise Black frees his game with . . . , P–KB4.

5.		N–N1
6.	B–Q3	B–K2
7.	N–B3	

More economical is 7 P–B4 and 8 N–B3.

7.		N–KB3
8.	N–K2	P–B3
9.	P–B4	N–R3
10.	N–N3	N–B4
11.	B–B2	P–QN4?!

With a view to breaking the grip of the White Pawns, but his pieces are not well posted for supporting the maneuver.

12.	P–N4!	N–N2
13.	QP×P	B×P
14.	P×P	B×NP

| 15. | P–QR4 | B–Q2 |
| 16. | O–O | P–N3 |

Black's game is cramped, he has a weak Queen Pawn and must contend with a hostile Queen-side majority of Pawns. He therefore concludes that he must try at all costs to get some sort of attack going.

17. P–R3?

This serves no positive purpose and creates a target for Black's future attack.

| 17. | | P–KR4 |
| 18. | B–K3 | P–R4!? |

Gaining the square QB4 for his Queen Knight, which is a more important consideration at this point than the fact that White's Queen Knight Pawn becomes passed.

| 19. | P–N5 | QR–B! |
| 20. | R–B1 | N–B4 |

Incidentally threatening to win the King Pawn with . . . , P–R5.

| 21. | N–Q2 | P–R5 |
| 22. | N–K2 | P–N4!? |

Desperate situations call for desperate remedies, and

70

Blackburne decides to sacrifice a Pawn to further his attack.

23.   B×P

23 P—B3 is safer, but then the position takes on a barricaded aspect that is not propitious for White's winning purposes.

23.   KR—N1
24.   B×P?

But this is altogether too provocative, as the complete opening of the King Rook file gives Black a really dangerous attack.

24 B×N, B×B; 25 K—R1 is the safe course; but in this game, Lasker consistently despises safety.

24.	B×RP
25. B—KN3	B—K3
26. R—K1	N—N5!
27. N—B1	B—N4!
28. R—N1	

If White appreciated the full force of the attack that Black has conjured out of a lost position, he would play 28 P—B4, though even then 28 . . . , B—R5 gives Black a powerful offensive.

28.   R—KR1!
29.   N—B3?

His last hope of possibly repulsing the attack is 29 P—B4.

29.   B—KB5!
30.   N—Q5

If 30 B×B, Black plays 30 . . . , Q—R5!, although he also has 30 . . . , R—R8ch.!

Black's attack is now beginning to show in its true colors.

30.   Q—N4!
31.   P—B3

Forced by the threat of Q—R4.

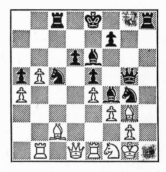

31.   R—R8ch.!!

The brilliant culmination of a fighting recovery.

32.   K×R   B×B
33.   N×B

If 33 R—K2 (against . . . , N—B7ch.), Black wins by 33 . . . , Q—R5ch.; 34 K—N1, B—R7ch.!, and now 35 K—R1, N—B7ch.!!; 36 R×N, B—N6ch.; 37 K—N1, B×R mate, or 35 N×B, Q×Nch.; 36 K—B1, Q—R8 mate.

Of course, 33 P×N?? allows mate in two.

33.	N—B7ch.
34. K—N1	N×Q
35. N—B5	B×N/B4
36. P×B	Q—Q7

As a result of his combination, Black has a Queen for Rook, with an easy win. But Lasker still has some fight left in him.

37.	KR×N	Q×B
38.	QR—B1	Q×BP
39.	N—N6	R—Q1
40.	N—B4	N—N2
41.	N—K3	Q—B5
42.	K—B2	Q×P
43.	R—B7	N—B4
44.	R—KR1	

Threatening mate on the move, a wonderful achievement after his hopeless position of eight moves earlier.

44.		R—Q2
45.	R—B8ch.	K—K2
46.	R/R1—R8	

Making a last brave effort.
If now 46 . . . , Q×P? White even now escapes with a draw by 47 R/B8—K8ch., K—B3; 48 N—N4ch., K—B4 (if 48 . . . ,

K—N4; 49 R/R8—N8ch.); 49 N—K3ch., K—B3 (if 49 . . . , K—B5; 50 P—N3ch., K—N4; 51 R/R8—N8ch.); 50 N—N4ch., etc.

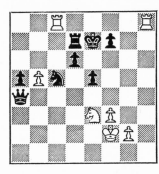

46.		Q—Q5!
	Resigns	

White's Knight is pinned, ruling out the perpetual check. A great game, Lasker's only loss in the tournament and one that earned Blackburne the brilliancy prize.

Janowski—Burn

MUNICH, 1900

David Janowski (1868–1927), a Pole by birth but French by adoption, was with Marshall regarded as the rising star of the beginning of the twentieth century. Eventually he achieved a match with Lasker for the world title, but was heavily defeated.

RUY LOPEZ

White	Black
Janowski	Burn
1. P–K4	P–K4
2. N–KB3	N–QB3
3. B–N5	N–B3
4. O–O	N×P
5. P–Q4	N–Q3
6. B–R4!?	

An unusual move, to which the best reply is 6 . . . , P–K5.

6.	P×P
7. P–B3!	

A bold line by which he hopes to take advantage of the poor position of the Black Knights. If Black replies 7 . . . , P×P then 8 N×P, B–K2; 9 N–Q5, O–O; 10 B–B4, with strong pressure. Black prefers to return the Pawn.

7.	B–K2
8. P×P	P–QN4!

An elaborate but ultimately effective freeing maneuver.

9. B–N3	N–R4
10. B–B2	B–N2
11. N–K5	O–O
12. N–QB3	N/R4–B5?!

As this loses the Queen Knight Pawn, the more solid 12 . . . , P–QR3 is preferable.

13. P–QN3	N–N3
14. N×NP!	N×N
15. Q–Q3	P–KB4
16. Q×N	P–QR4

Threatens . . . , B–R3.

17. Q–K2	B–Q4
18. R–K1	B–N5

With a few rapid strokes, Black completes his development but comes out with yet another indefensible Queen Knight Pawn.

19. B–Q2	Q–R5
20. B×B	P×B
21. Q–Q2	P–Q3
22. N–Q3	P–B5?!

The sound line is 22 . . . , Q×P; 23 Q×P, Q×Q; 24 N×Q, P–B4, with a drawish outlook. Burn prefers an enterprising if risky attack.

23. P–B3

23 Q×NP or 23 N×NP is too risky because of 23 . . . , P–B6.

| 23. | R—B4! |
| 24. Q—B2 | |

But not 24 N×NP, R—KR4; 25 P—KR3, B×BP!; 26 P×B, Q×P, with a winning attack.

24.	Q—R3
25. N×NP	R—KR4
26. P—KR3	R—KB1
27. P—QR4	

Threatening to win a piece with 28 P—R5.

27 N×B is not good because the Knight settles on K6.

| 27. | B—K3 |
| 28. P—R5 | |

28.   B×RP!?

Getting in the first blow in a very critical position and threatening . . . , R—KN4. Any less vigorous line to save the Knight allows White's Queen Rook Pawn to become a menace. If now 29 P×B, R×P, and wins.

| 29. P×N | P×P |
| 30. B—Q3 | |

Too late to defend his KN2.

| 30. | B×P |
| 31. Q×B | |

The Queen cannot be saved, so he plays to get three pieces for it.

31.	R—KN4
32. R—R2!	R×Qch.
33. R×R	Q—B3
34. N—B6!	

Black's attack is over, and now it is White who has the initiative again.

He now threatens 35 N—K7ch., K—R1; 36 N—N6ch., P×N; 37 R—R2ch., K—N1; 38 B—B4ch., winning the Queen.

| 34. | P—Q4 |
| 35. N—K7ch. | K—B2 |

On 35 . . . , K—R1; 36 B×P! is decisive.

36. R—K5	P—N3
37. N×QP	Q—Q1
38. R—K7ch.	K—N1

39. B—B4?

Missing the most conclusive line: 39 B×P!, P×B; 40 R×

Pch., K—R1; 41 R—R6ch., K—N1; 42 R/R6—R7, R—B2; 43 R/K7×R, Q×N; 44 R/B7—N7ch., K—B1; 45 R—Q7, Q—N4ch.; 46 K—B1, Q—N4ch.; 47 K—B2, K—N1; 48 R/Q7—N7ch., K—B1; 49 R—R7, K—N1; 50 R/KR7—N7, Q—K1; 51 R—N7ch., K—R1 (51 . . . , K—B1 results in a lost King and Pawn ending); 52 R—R7ch., K—N1; 53 R/QR7—N7ch., K—B1; 54 R—R8ch., etc. The variation is long, but virtually all of Black's moves are forced.

39.	K—R1
40. R—KR2	P—R4
41. R—K6?	

After this it is very questionable whether White can win. Keeping the Rook on the seventh rank is much stronger, but the immediate 41 R/R2—K2 can be answered by 41 . . . , P—QN4! Hence the right way is 41 P—N4! (assuring the Knight of lasting protection) to be followed by R/R2—K2.

41.	R—B4!

Better than 41 . . . , K—N2 (or 41 . . . , K—R2); 42 R—KN2.

Black now threatens to break the attack with . . . , R×N.

42. R/R2—K2	K—R2
43. R—K7ch.	K—R3
44. R—K8	

44 R/K2—K5 may be more promising.

44.	Q—R5
45. R—KN2	P—QN4!

Apparently succeeding at last in breaking up White's game with advantage. But White finds a brilliant continuation to the attack.

46. R—R8ch.!	K—N2
47. R—N8ch.!!	

The point! Black dare not reply 47 . . . , K×R? because of 48 N—K7ch., K—R2 (other moves lose the Queen); 49 B—N8ch., K—R3; 50 R×P mate!

47.	K—B2
48. R/N2×P	P×B

Black dare not try 48 . . . , Q—K8ch.; 49 K—R2, Q—B7ch.; 50 R—N2, Q×QP? because of 51 R/N2—N7ch., K—K3 (if 51 . . . , Q×R; 52 N—K7ch.! wins); 52 R—K7ch., K—Q3; 53 R—Q8ch., K—B4; 54 R—B7 mate.

After the text move, White must take the draw.

49. R/N8—N7ch.	

For now 49 R/N6—N7ch.? fails because the King can take the Knight after . . . , K—K3.

49.	K—K1
50. R—N8ch.	K—B2
51. R/N8—N7ch.	K—B1
52. R—N8ch.	K—B2
Drawn	

A tremendous game.

Marshall—Pillsbury

Frank J. Marshall (1877–1945) was famous for his bold style of play. He never missed an opportunity for enterprising, imaginative sacrifices. Marshall became United States champion in 1909 by winning a match from Showalter, and held the title until 1936, when he relinquished it to the younger generation of American masters. In tournament competition, his greatest successes were at Cambridge Springs, 1904, and Nuremberg, 1906.

KING'S GAMBIT

White	Black
Marshall	Pillsbury
1. P–K4	P–K4
2. P–KB4	P×P

In this tournament, the offer and acceptance of the gambit were obligatory.

3. N–KB3	P–KN4
4. B–B4	B–N2
5. P–KR4	P–KR3
6. P–Q4	P–Q3
7. Q–Q3	P–N5!?

The advance of the King-side Pawn leads to dangerous play for both sides.

8. N–N1	Q–B3
9. P–B3	P–KR4
10. N–QR3	N–K2
11. N–K2	N–N3
12. P–KN3!	P×P

Apparently very risky, but 12 . . . , P–B6? gives Black a bad game because of 13 B–N5!

13. R–B1?!

A daring move quite in Marshall's style. He sees that after 13 Q×P Black has a simple defense in 13 . . . , B–K3. Hence the text is played in order to keep the attack alive—at considerable material cost.

13.	Q×RP
14. B×Pch.	K–Q1
15. B×N	P–N7ch.
16. R–B2	R–B1!
17. B–K3	B–R3!

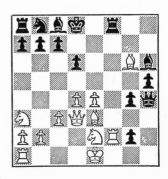

Marshall's faith in the attack must indeed be profound, to allow such a position to arise! Marco indicates the following unwelcome possibilities:

a) 18 N—KN1, R—B6!! and wins.

b) 18 B—B5, QB×B; 19 P× B, R—K1! and wins.

c) 18 O—O—O, B×Bch.; 19 Q×B, Q×R, with advantage to Black.

18.	B×B!?	P—N8(Q)ch.
19.	N×Q	Q×Rch.
20.	K—Q1	Q×Nch.
21.	K—B2	R—B7ch.
22.	B—Q2	Q×R

Despite his enormous lead in material, Black's game is far from easy. His backward development may yet tell against him.

23.	Q—K3	R×Bch.
24.	Q×R	B—Q2

Good enough, although . . . , P—B3 gives an easier defense.

25.	Q—N5ch.	K—B1
26.	B—B5!	P—N3!

Playing to win, he spurns the draw that would result from 26 . . . , B×B; 27 Q—N8ch., etc.

27.	Q—N8ch.	K—N2
28.	B×B	N×B
29.	Q—Q5ch.	P—B3

The simplest winning method is 29 . . . , K—N1; 30

Q—N8ch., N—B1!; 31 Q×Nch., K—N2, etc.

30.	Q×QP	R—Q1
31.	P—Q5!?	

The only chance to complicate matters. Who would believe that White will yet win this game?!

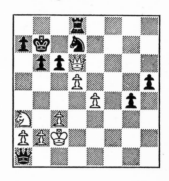

31.		R—KB1?

This plausible move loses, as Black's counterattack proves futile.

The right way was 31 . . . , N—B4!!; 32 Q×R, Q—B8!!; 33 P×Pch., K×P, and Black's passed Pawns will prevail, as White has no perpetual check.

32.	P×Pch.	K—R1
33.	P×N	R—B7ch.
34.	K—N3	Q×NPch.
35.	K—R4	Resigns

For if 35 . . . , P—N4ch.; 36 K—R5, Q×Pch.; 37 K—R6. One of the most fascinating games ever played!

GAME 22

Lasker—Napier

CAMBRIDGE SPRINGS, 1904

William E. Napier (born 1881) was taken from England to America as a child, and in 1908 he became an American citizen. He was known as a child prodigy and won the championship of the Brooklyn Chess Club at the age of 15. In 1904 he won the British Championship, but in the following year retired absolutely from the game. His contributions to chess literature reveal him as a writer of great distinction and charm.

SICILIAN DEFENSE

	White Lasker	Black Napier
1.	P–K4	P–QB4
2.	N–QB3	N–QB3
3.	N–B3	P–KN3
4.	P–Q4	P×P
5.	N×P	B–N2
6.	B–K3	P–Q3
7.	P–KR3	N–B3
8.	P–KN4!?	

An advance justified not by the position but by Lasker's own ability. Black's attempt to disprove the move leads to a game of enthralling complexity.

8.		O–O!?
9.	P–N5	N–K1
10.	P–KR4	N–B2
11.	P–B4	P–K4!
12.	KN–K2	P–Q4?!

Overestimating his position, though the ensuing course of the game shows that Black had plausible reasons for believing that by this move he would secure the advantage. Correct is 12 . . . , B–N5!

13.	KP×P	N–Q5

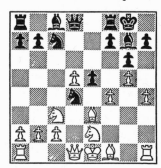

14. N×N!

If 14 B×N, P×B; 15 N×P, N×P; 16 Q–Q2, R–K1ch.; 17 B–K2, N×P recovering the Pawn with the better game.

14. N×P!

Beginning to force White's hand.

15 N×N is no reply now as 15 . . . , P×N wins after 16 B×P, Q×N; 17 B×B, Q×R; 18 B×R, Q×Pch., etc.

78

15. N–B5!!   N×N!!

The only way to parry White's threat to win a piece.

16. Q×Q

If 16 P×N, B×N; 17 P×P, B×KP; 18 B–Q4, B–N6ch.; 19 B–B2 (not 19 K–Q2?, Q–Q4; 20 KR–N1, B–B5ch.), Q–B2, with the better game.

16.   R×Q
17. N–K7ch.!

If 17 N×B, N–Q4; 18 O–O–O, B–N5! and White cannot play 19 R–Q3?, for then 19 . . . , N×B; 20 R×N, R–Q8 mate.

Also if 17 P×N, B×N; 18 P×P, B×P; 19 B–Q2, B–N6ch., with advantage to Black.

The shrewdness of Black's calculation on his 12th move is becoming apparent, and White must find the very best move every time to escape defeat. But at the same time White is quietly preparing his own plans against the Black King, as will soon appear.

17.   K–R1!

Avoiding the trap 17 . . . , K–B1?; 18 N×B, N–Q4; 19 B–B5ch., and Black loses a piece.

[*See diagram in next column.*]

18. P–R5!!

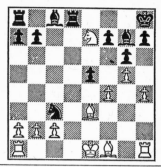

In his increasingly difficult position, White exercises every subtlety to elude disaster.

18 P×N, so far from winning a piece, actually loses by 18 . . . , P×P!; 19 B–Q4, B×B; 20 P×B, R–K1!

As for 18 N×B, the reply 18 . . . , N–Q4! retains for Black his material and positional advantage.

White's last move, despite its inconsequential appearance, initiates what turns out to be the decisive attack. The immediate threat is 19 RP×P, BP×P; 20 N×Pch., K–N1; 21 B–B4ch., N–Q4; 22 B×Nch., R×B; 23 N–K7ch., winning the Rook.

18.   R–K1
19. B–B5!   NP×P!

It is Black who must now take care not to lose a piece. If 19 . . . , KP×P; 20 P×P!, P×P; 21 B–B4!! threatening 22 B–B7!

And if 19 . . . , N–K5; 20 RP×P, BP×P; 21 B–N5!, B–B4 (not 21 . . . , R–Q1; 22 N×Pch., K–N1; 23 B–B4ch.

followed by mate); 22 B×R, R×B (not 22 . . . , N×B; 23 B×P); 23 N×B, N×B; 24 N× B, and wins.

The unlikely text move is the apparent solution to his problem: he will sacrifice the exchange in the hope of obtaining a draw with his two Bishops.

20. **B—B4!!**

20 P×N, B—B1; 21 B—N5, R×N; 22 B×R, B×B offers Black excellent drawing prospects.

White, who has throughout accepted all Black's challenges, prefers to continue his threats to the Black King.

20.   **P×P?!**

The alternative, holding out more drawing chances, was 20 . . . , B—K3; 21 B×B, P×B; 22 P×N, B—B1; 23 R×P, B× N; 24 B×B, R×B; 25 P×P, R—QB1; 26 O—O—O, R×P; 27 P—N6.

But Black has yet another surprise by which he hopes to win!

21. **B×BP!**	**N—K5!!**
22. **B×R**	**B×P**
23. **QR—N1**	**B—B6ch.**
24. **K—B1**	**B—KN5!**

The key move of Black's plan. White is faced with no less than four threats: . . . , R×B; . . . , N×B; . . . , N—Q7ch.; . . . , N—N6ch.

White must return his material advantage, for a move like

25 K—N2 simply creates another threat in the advance of Black's Bishop Pawn. But Lasker simplifies neatly.

25. **B×KRP!**	**B×B**
26. **R×B!**	**N—N6ch.**
27. **K—N2**	**N×R**
28. **R×P**	

The complications are over, and the material is still level. It will be seen, however, that White's position is now superior.

28.	**P—R4**
29. **R—N3!**	**B—N2**
30. **R—KR3!**	**N—N6**
31. **K—B3!**	

And now White secures his first clear material advantage, one Pawn.

31 . . . , B—K4? is now answered by 32 N—N6ch.—but more deadly to Black is the threat of P—N6.

31.	**R—R3**
32. **K×P**	**N—K7ch.**
33. **K—B5**	**N—B6**
34. **P—R3**	**N—R5**
35. **B—K3**	**Resigns**

It is rare indeed that two masters, both with considerable justification, play to outcombine one another in the same combination.

In *Lasker's Chess Career* may be found this well-deserved comment: "One of the most beautiful, most profound, most exciting, and most difficult games in the whole literature of chess!"

Duras—Teichmann

OSTEND, 1906

Oldrich Duras (born 1882) was a brilliant Czech player of the first decade of the twentieth century. He won tournaments against the strongest opposition, notably sharing first prize in the Prague and Vienna tournaments of 1908. After 1914, he retired from active play.

Richard Teichmann (1868–1925), a German who lived for many years in England, promised at one time to become one of the world's strongest masters, but eye trouble forced him to abandon the practice of the game. His greatest success was winning first prize in the formidable tournament at Carlsbad, 1911.

RUY LOPEZ

	White	Black
	Duras	Teichmann
1.	P–K4	P–K4
2.	N–KB3	N–QB3
3.	B–N5	P–QR3
4.	B–R4	N–B3
5.	O–O	B–K2
6.	R–K1	P–Q3
7.	P–B3	O–O
8.	P–KR3	P–R3

Beginning a long-winded rearrangement of his forces that is characteristic of this rather restricted variation.

9.	P–Q4	B–Q2
10.	QN–Q2	R–K1
11.	N–B1	B–KB1
12.	N–N3	P–KN3
13.	B–N3	Q–K2
14.	B–K3	B–N2

The purpose of White's last move becomes apparent if Black plays 14 . . . , N–QR4:

for then 15 P×P, P×P; 16 N×P, N×B; 17 P×N, Q×N; 18 B–Q4, Q–K2; 19 B×N, Q×B; 20 Q×B, winning a Pawn.

15.	P–Q5	N–Q1
16.	P–B4	P–N3
17.	B–B2	P–QR4
18.	N–R2	K–R2
19.	R–N1	N–N1
20.	P–B4	

After a typical Lopez period of preparation, Black now has to make up his mind how to deal with White's first aggressiveness. If he does not capture the Pawn, he may be faced with either 21 P–B5, or 21 N–B3 and 22 P×P. In the latter case he has to recapture on K4 with the Black Pawn on Q3, and then White's Queen side suddenly assumes a much more menacing aspect after P–QR3, P–QN4, and P–QB4–5.

20.		P×P
21.	B×BP	B—K4

To permit an eventual P—K5 would be to allow the full force of White's attack to develop against his King. By exchanging Bishops and getting his Queen off the King file, the threat is largely diminished.

22.	B×B	Q×B
23.	N—K2	Q—N2
24.	N—KB3	N—N2
25.	N—N3	N—B4
26.	Q—Q2	R—K2
27.	Q—B2	QR—K1

It has been suggested that 28 P—K5 must be prevented not for positional but for combinative reasons, the continuation given being 28 . . . , P×P; 29 N—R5, Q—R1; 30 R×P, R×R; 31 N—N5ch., P×N; 32 Q× Pch. followed by mate.

However, there seems no valid objection to 29 . . . , Q—B1, beyond the fact that White's position has been improved by the Pawn advance.

28.	R—K2	K—R1
29.	P—N3	N—B3
30.	QR—K1	N—R2
31.	B—N1	N—N4
32.	N×N	

Double-edged. He will now have to prevent . . . , P—N5, and this lets the Queen take up a strong position on the black squares. In addition, it gives Black an open file against the White King.

| 32. | | P×N |

33.	Q—B3	Q—Q5ch.
34.	K—R2	K—N2
35.	R—KB2	

To give his King a flight square on KN1 after 35 . . . , P—N5; 36 P×P, R—R1ch.

35.		Q—K4
36.	R/K1—KB1	R—KR1
37.	K—N1	R—R5
38.	Q—K3	R—R3

The inviting 38 . . . , P—N5 is most effectively answered by 39 R—B4! with advantage to White.

This is clearer than the complicated line (after 38 . . . , P—N5) 39 N—B5ch.!?, B×N; 40 R×B!?, P×R; 41 Q—N5ch., K—B1; 42 Q×R, BP×P; 43 R—B6 (threatening mate), K—K1; 44 Q×P, etc. Black lifts the mating threat with 44 . . . , K—Q1, and his chances are at least as good as White's.

39.	P—R3	P—N5
40.	P×P	B×P
41.	R—B4	B—Q2
42.	Q—B2	B—K1

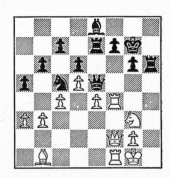

43. **R—B5?!**

The brilliant but unsound beginning of a brilliant but inaccurately executed combination!

43.		**Q—B6?**

Correct is 43 . . . , P×R!; 44 N×Pch., K—R2; 45 N×R/ R6, K×N; 46 Q—R4ch., K—N2 (not 46 . . . , Q—R4?; 47 R—B6ch., winning the Queen); 47 R—B3, P—KB3!! and White's attack is bankrupt.

Note, on the other hand, that after the careless 47 . . . , N×KP?; 48 B×N, Q×B; 49 R—N3ch. is decisive.

44. **P—K5!**

Now the attack will succeed: White opens up the diagonal for his Bishop and simultaneously shuts off Black's Queen from the defense.

44.	**P×P**
45. R—N5	**K—R2**
46. N—B5!!	

Very fine. He forces the pace with a move that Black had actually taken steps to prevent.

46.	**P×N**
47. Q×Pch.	**R—N3**

Unsatisfactory, as is also the most likely alternative 47 . . . , K—R1; 48 R—R5, Q—K6ch.; 49 K—R2:

a) 49 . . . , N—Q2; 50 R—B3, Q—Q7; 51 R×Rch., Q×R; 52 R—R3 winning the Queen.

b) 49 . . . , P—K5; 50 Q—B6ch., K—R2 (if 50 . . . , K—N1; 51 R×R); 51 R/B1—B5, R—Q2; 52 R/B5—N5, again winning the Queen.

48. **Q—B6!**

With the triple threat of 49 R—R5ch., 49 B×Rch., and 49 Q×R/K7. Black fights desperately to stave off these threats.

48.	**Q—Q5ch.**
49. R—B2	**Q—Q8ch.**
50. K—R2	**P—K5**

51. **Q×R?**

51 R×R wins a full Rook! Thus if 51 . . . , P×R; 52 Q×Rch., etc.; and if instead 51 . . . , Q—R4ch.; 52 K—N1 and Black's remaining Rook falls by the wayside.

51.	**R—R3ch.**
52. K—N3	**Q—K8!**

Much stronger than 52 . . . , Q×NPch.; 53 R—B3. The threat 53 . . . , Q—K6ch. puts both White Rooks in jeopardy.

53. Q×B!	**Q—K6ch.**
54. K—N4	**P—B4ch.!**

Of course not 54 . . . , Q×R?; 55 Q—N8 mate.

Against the text move, White must be careful. If 55 K×P?, Q×R/B7ch., and mates next move; while if 55 R/B2×P? there is perpetual check by 55 . . . , Q—K7ch.; 56 K—B4 (if 56 K—N3, Q—K6ch.), Q—B7ch.; 57 K—K5, Q—N7ch., etc.

55. R/N5×P!   R—N3ch.
56. Q×Rch.!

The climax of Black's attempt at counterplay.

White cannot play 56 K—R4?? because of 56 . . . , Q—N6ch.; 57 K—R5, R—R3 mate. So he must give up Queen for Rook. But his two Rooks are in co-operation and will be strong enough to win.

56.		K×Q
57.	R—B6ch.	K—N2
58.	R—B7ch.	K—N1
59.	R—B8ch.	K—N2
60.	R/B2—B7ch.	K—N3
61.	R—B6ch.	K—N2
62.	R/B8—B7ch.	K—N1
63.	K—R5!!	

Threatening mate in two.

63.		Q—K7ch.
64.	P—N4	Resigns

If 64 . . . , Q—R7ch.; 65 K—N6, and there are no more checks. An absorbing example of attack and defense.

GAME 24

Rubinstein—Lasker

ST. PETERSBURG, 1909

Akiba Rubinstein (born 1882), a Pole by birth, came rapidly into prominence early in the 1900's. His style was quiet and simple but always extremely effective. Frequent tournament successes, such as first prizes at Carlsbad, 1907, and San Sebastian and Pistyan, 1912, and his tie for first prize with Lasker at St. Petersburg, 1909, brought him into consideration as a challenger for the world title, but he never secured a match. He retired in 1930 suffering with a breakdown from which he has never fully recovered.

QUEEN'S GAMBIT
DECLINED

White	Black
Rubinstein	Lasker
1. P—Q4	P—Q4
2. N—KB3	N—KB3
3. P—B4	P—K3
4. B—N5	P—B4?!

An inferior move that comes better after 4 N—B3, as he can then continue 4 . . . , P—B4; 5 B—N5, BP×P; 6 KN×P, P—K4.

As the game actually goes, Black is left with a weak, isolated Queen Pawn.

5. BP×P	KP×P
6. N—B3	P×P
7. KN×P	N—B3!

The complications begin. The text invites 8 B×N, Q×B; 9 N×P, Q×N; 10 N—B7ch., K—Q1; 11 N×R, B—N5ch., and Black wins.

| 8. P—K3 | B—K2 |

| 9. B—N5 | B—Q2 |

"Rubinstein sees now that he can win the Pawn at Q5," Reti comments, "but in order to do so must undergo an apparently irresistible attack. This attack which Black will obtain looks so dangerous that even players known for their boldness would not have ventured to take the Pawn."

10. B×KN!	B×B
11. N×P	B×N
12. P×B	Q—N4!

The point: 13 N—B7ch., K—Q1 favors Black:

a) 14 N×R, Q×B; 15 Q—N3, R—K1ch.; 16 K—Q1, Q—K7ch.; 17 K—B1, N×P; 18 Q—QB3, Q×P!; 19 Q—B7ch., K—K2, and wins.

b) 14 N×R, Q×B; 15 Q—B2, R—K1ch.; 16 K—Q1, N×P; 17 Q—B7ch., K—K2; 18 R—K1ch., N—K3, and Black must win.

c) 14 B×N, B×B; 15 P—Q5, K×N; 16 P×B, QR—Q1; 17 Q—B2, KR—K1ch.; 18 K—B1, Q—N4ch., with the better game.

13. **B×N**   **B×B**

"This open and beautiful position which Lasker has attained in a few moves in the defense of a Queen's Gambit is indeed an admirable example of his genius for positions."—Reti.

14. **N—K3**

But of course not 14 N—B7ch.??, K—Q2; 15 N×R, R—K1ch.; 16 K—B1, Q×P mate.

14.   **O—O—O!?**

This leads to exceptionally critical play, but the alternative line is much in White's favor: 14 . . . , B×P; 15 KR—N1, Q—R4ch.; 16 Q—Q2, Q×Qch.; 17 K×Q, B—K5; 18 R—N4! B—N3; 19 P—B4!, P—B4; 20 R—N2, and White's passed Pawn is a tower of strength—not to mention the manifestly superior position of his pieces.

15. **O—O!**   **KR—K1!**

At first sight, this move seems to leave White without resource, for if now 16 P—KN3?, R×N!; 17 P×R, Q×KPch.; 18 R—B2, Q—K5!; 19 R—K2, Q—R8ch., etc.

Or 16 P—B4, Q—N3; 17 Q—N4ch., and White is left with a vastly inferior ending.

16. **R—B1!**

One of the deepest moves in the history of chess!

16.   **R×N!?**

Threatening 17 . . . , Q×P mate.

Black has brought all his forces into play in the minimum of time, and White will have great difficulty in preventing him from equalizing.

16 . . . , K—N1 fails after 17 R—B5!, Q—B5 (or 17 . . . , Q—N3; 18 P—Q5 beating off the attack with a Pawn to the good); 18 P—Q5, R×N; 19 Q—B1!!, R—K5; 20 P×B, P×P; 21 Q—B3 with advantage to White.

17. **R×Bch.**   **P×R**

Now White seems to have nothing better than 18 P×R?, Q×KPch., when Black wins the Queen Pawn with a fine game.

18. **Q—B1!!**

The climax of White's magnificent plan. The complications are considerable even though all the minor pieces are gone.

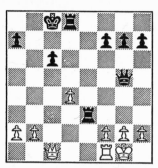

If Black defends his Queen Bishop Pawn, White takes the Rook and remains a Pawn ahead.

18.   R×P!?

White has a harder win after 18 . . . , R—K4!; 19 Q×Pch. (if 19 P—B4, R—QB4!), K—N1; 20 P×R (if 20 P—B4, R—K3!; 21 Q×R, Q×Pch.!), Q×P; 21 R—B1, Q—Q3 etc.

19.   P×R!

After 19 Q×Pch., K—N1 there are no more checks and White must continue 20 P×R, Q×KPch.; 21 K—R1, Q—K7; 22 R—KN1 (there are astonishingly enough still no checks), R—Q8, and the draw is almost inevitable.

But White has no intention of letting Black get the draw.

19.   R—Q2

Or 19 . . . , R—Q3; 20 R×P and White has much the better game.

20.   Q×Pch.   K—Q1

Not 20 . . . , R—B2; 21 Q—R8ch., K—Q2; 22 R×Pch., K—K3; 23 Q—K8ch.! K—Q3; 24 R×R, winning.

21.   R—B4!

The manner in which Rubinstein combines attack and defense hereabouts is truly admirable.

The text move wards off the attack on the King Pawn and at the same time threatens Q—R8ch. followed by R—K4ch. with fatal consequences for Black.

21.   P—B4

Both players fight all the way.

If instead 21 . . . , R—Q8ch.; 22 K—B2, R—Q7ch.; 23 K—K1, Q×P; 24 R—Q4ch.!, K—K2; 25 Q—Q6ch., and mate next move.

22.   Q—B5!

At last White establishes his advantage.

Black cannot defend the Bishop Pawn by 22 . . . , P—N3 because of 23 Q—B8ch., K—B2; 24 R—B4ch., K—N3; 25 Q—N4ch., K—R3; 26 R—B6 mate.

Nor is 22 . . . , R—Q8ch.; 23 K—B2, R—Q7ch.; 24 K—K1, Q×P, feasible because of 25 Q—R5ch., winning the Rook.

22.		Q—K2
23.	Q×Qch.	K×Q
24.	R×P	R—Q8ch.
25.	K—B2!	R—Q7ch.
26.	K—B3	R×QNP
27.	R—QR5!	

He has come through a harassing time into a won Rook ending. There are, however, so many positions in Rook endings where the extra Pawn does not win that he still has to be very careful how he forces the position.

27.		R—N2
28.	R—R6!	K—B1

Black can only mark time.

29.	P—K4	R—B2
30.	P—KR4	

White advances his Kingside Pawns in order to weaken the hostile Pawn position.

30.		K—B2
31.	P—N4	K—B1
32.	K—B4	K—K2
33.	P—R5!	

Black can no longer avoid weakening his position. Thus if 33 . . . , K—B2; 34 K—B5, K—K2; 35 P—K5, K—B2; 36 P—N5, K—K2; 37 P—R6!, P×P (or 37 . . . , P—N3ch.; 38 K—

K4 etc.); 38 P×P, and Black will soon be in *Zugzwang*.

33.		P—R3
34.	K—B5	K—B2
35.	P—K5	R—N2
36.	R—Q6!	K—K2

Or 36 . . . , R—K2; 37 R—Q7!, R×R; 38 P—K6ch., K—K2; 39 P×R, K×P; 40 K—N6, and the King and Pawn ending is child's play for White.

37.	R—R6	K—B2
38.	R—Q6	K—B1
39.	R—B6	

Another way is 39 R—Q8ch. and 40 R—QR8.

39.		K—B2
40.	P—R3!	Resigns

A delightful conclusion to a classic ending.

Black has no adequate reply, for example:

a) 40 . . . , K—K2; 41 K—N6, K—B1; 42 R—B8ch., K—K2; 43 R—KN8, and wins.

b) 40 . . . , R—K2; 41 P—K6ch., K—N1; 42 R—B8ch., K—R2; 43 K—K5, followed by K—Q6, winning.

c) 40 . . . , K—B1; 41 K—N6, R—Q2; 42 R—B8ch., K—K2; 43 R—KN8, R—Q5 (or 43 . . . , K—K3; 44 R—K8ch.); 44 R×Pch., K—K3; 45 K×P, with two united passed Pawns.

GAME 25

Marshall—Capablanca

MATCH, 1909

José Raul Capablanca (1888–1942), a Cuban, began playing as a child, was champion of Cuba at the age of twelve, of the Americas at twenty-one, and of the world at thirty-three. His style was simple and almost mechanical, of an accuracy that reduced opponents to despair. He won a series of tournament victories from 1910 to 1936, and it was only after he lost the world title in 1927 that his infallibility was called into question.

QUEEN'S GAMBIT
DECLINED

	White	Black
	Marshall	Capablanca
1.	P–Q4	P–Q4
2.	P–QB4	P–K3
3.	N–QB3	N–KB3
4.	B–N5	B–K2
5.	P–K3	N–K5

A defense taken over by Capablanca from Lasker for this match. Its great virtue is simplification.

| 6. | B×B | Q×B |
| 7. | B–Q3 | |

This allows Black to open the long diagonal for his remaining Bishop.

7.		N×N
8.	P×N	P×P!
9.	B×BP	P–QN3
10.	Q–B3	

He cannot hold the diagonal, but this move leads to more combinative possibilities than the usual N–B3.

10.		P–QB3
11.	N–K2	B–N2
12.	O–O	O–O
13.	P–QR4	

To prevent 13 . . . , P–QN4; 14 B–Q3, P–QB4; 15 Q–N3, P–B5; 16 B–B2, P–QR4 with strong expansionist tendencies on the Queen side. Nevertheless, the move is risky. 13 P–K4 is safer and yet more aggressive.

13.		P–QB4
14.	Q–N3	N–B3
15.	N–B4	QR–B1
16.	B–R2	

Black was threatening to win a Pawn by . . . , P×P, etc. After the text, White's Queen Rook Pawn is hardly tenable, but 16 B–N3 is unsatisfactory because of 16 . . . , N–R4.

16.		KR–Q1
17.	KR–K1	N–R4
18.	QR–Q1	

As it would be awkward to defend the weak Queen Rook

Pawn, White decides to sacrifice it if need be, gaining time for a push in the center.

18.   **B–B3**

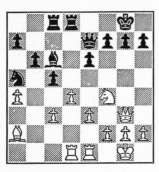

19. **Q–N4?!**

This leads to an amazingly virulent attack, but 19 P–Q5! is even stronger. The quiet rejoinder 19 . . . , P×P; 20 N×P, B×N; 21 B×B, gives White somewhat the better game because of his splendidly centralized Bishop.

But real fireworks ensue after 19 P–Q5! if Black tries 19 . . . , B×RP?; 20 P×P! with these possibilities:

a) 20 . . . , B×R; 21 P× Pch., K–R1; 22 N–N6ch.!, P× N; 23 P–B3!! and Black can resign.

b) 20 . . . , R×R; 21 P× Pch., K–B1 (21 . . . , K–R1 allows mate in three); 22 R× R, B×R; 23 Q–N6!! leaving Black without a defense.

19.   **P–B5**

If at once 19 . . . , B×RP; 20 N×P, P×N; 21 B×Pch., K–

R1; 22 B×R, B×R; 23 R×B, and it is White who is a Pawn ahead.

20. **P–Q5**

An interesting alternative is 20 P–K4, B×RP; 21 N–R5, P–N3; 22 P–K5, B×R; 23 R× B, threatening N–B6ch. followed by Q–R4.

20.   **B×RP?**

This leads to an arduous defense. Simpler and more convincing is 20 . . . , P×P; 21 N×P, B×N; 22 R×B, R×R; 23 Q×Rch., R–Q1; 24 Q–B5, P–N3; 25 Q–B2, Q–Q3, with a view to . . . , Q–Q7, when Black will have a strategically won game.

21. **R–Q2**   **P–K4**

He must either submit to an attack on his King, or by playing . . . , P×P allow White freedom in the center.

22. **N–R5**   **P–N3**

He cannot avoid this weakening move, for if 22 . . . , Q– B1; 23 B–N1 and 23 . . . , P–N3 must follow; for 23 . . . , R–Q3 (preventing N– B6ch.) is answered by 24 N×P!

23. **P–Q6!**   **Q–K3**
24. **Q–N5**

Exchange of Queens would of course put an end to White's attacking chances, leaving him with a lost ending.

24.   **K–R1**

And not 24 . . . , R×P??;
25 R×R, Q×R; 26 Q–R6, Q–
B1; 27 N–B6ch., and mate
next move.

25.	N–B6	R×P
26.	R×R	Q×R
27.	B–N1	

27 Q–R4 is answered by 27
. . . , K–N2.

27.		N–B3
28.	B–B5!	R–Q1

28 . . . , P×B?? permits 29
Q–R6, winning.

| 29. | P–R4? |

29 B–Q7! was stronger: 29
. . . , Q–B1! (if 29 . . . , R×
B?; 30 Q–R6 wins); 30 Q–R4,
K–N2; 31 N–R5ch.!, P×N; 32
Q–N5ch., K–R1; 33 B×N,
B×B; 34 Q–B6ch. with per-
petual check.

29.		N–K2
30.	N–K4	Q–B2
31.	Q–B6ch.	K–N1
32.	B–K6!?	P×B

White continues to attack
with ingenuity, and the defense has to be a model of
fighting carefulness. If 32 . . . ,
R–KB1; 33 N–N5, P×B; 34
Q×Rch., K×Q; 35 N×Pch.,
winning the exchange.

33.	Q×KPch.	K–B1
34.	N–N5	N–N1
35.	P–B4	R–K1?

This leads to new difficulties. 35 . . . , B–K1 is best.

36. **P×P!**

The attack seems to have
been beaten off, but White
evolves still more surprises.
Black still comes out the exchange down if he takes the
Queen.

36.		R–K2
37.	R–B1ch.	K–N2
38.	P–R5!	B–K1!
39.	P–R6ch.!	K–R1!

If 39 . . . , N×P??; 40 Q–
B6ch. forces mate.
Or if 39 . . . , K×P??; 40
Q–N4!, K–N2; 41 N–K6ch.,
winning the exchange.

| 40. | Q–Q6 | Q–B4! |

The attack continues. If
instead 40 . . . , Q×Q?; 41
P×Q:
  a) 41 . . . , R–Q2; 42 R–
B8, R×P; 43 R×B winning.
  b) 41 . . . , R–K4; 42 P–
Q7!, B×P; 43 N–B7 mate.
  c) 41 . . . , R×P; 42 P–Q7!
winning at once.

| 41. | Q–Q4! |

If 41 Q×Q, P×Q; 42 R—B8, R×P; 43 N—B3, R×P; 44 N—N5, R—K4; 45 N—B3, R—K2; 46 N—N5, B—B3, and wins.

41.   **R×P!**

He must stop P—K6ch.; but if 41 . . . , Q×P; 42 R—B8!, Q×Q (forced by the threat of 43 R×B); 43 KP×Q, B—B3; 44 N—B7ch., R×N; 45 R×R, N×P; 46 R×P, with good drawing chances.

42.   **Q—Q7!?**

42 R—B7 was his best try, and if 42 . . . , N×P; 43 R×Pch., K—N1; 44 R—N7ch.!,

K×R; 45 N—K6ch., winning Black's Queen with slight drawing chances.

42.   **R—K2!**

The defense holds out against White's last brilliant fling. Fatal would be 42 . . . , B×Q??; 43 N—B7 mate!

43. **R—B7**   **B×Q**
        Resigns

A perfect demonstration of the power of even an unsound attack and of the inexorable justice that must come if the defense is correct.

Schlechter–Lasker

WORLD CHAMPIONSHIP MATCH, 1910

Carl Schlechter (1873–1918), of Vienna, early earned the unenviable title of "drawing master," though at his best he was as fine a stylist as any player of his time. However, when he shared first prize both at Vienna and Prague in 1908, after taking a clear first prize in the great tournament at Ostend in 1906, he was recognized for the great player he was. In 1910 he drew a match for the world title, and oddly enough he failed to win by spurning the draw in the last game of the match. Under-nourishment brought on by wartime conditions contributed to his death in 1918.

SICILIAN DEFENSE

White	Black
Schlechter	Lasker
1. P–K4	P–QB4
2. N–KB3	N–QB3
3. P–Q4	P×P
4. N×P	N–B3
5. N–QB3	P–KN3

Leads to unpleasant complications, which can be avoided by the more accurate 5 . . . , P–Q3.

6. B–QB4	P–Q3
7. N×N	P×N
8. P–K5!	

The point of this variation, named after its founder, Magnus Smith. If now 8 . . . , P× P??; 9 B×Pch.! wins the Queen.

8.	N–N5
9. P–K6	P–KB4
10. O–O	B–KN2

Black's position is difficult;

thus, if 10 . . . , P–Q4?; 11 N×P!, P×N?; 12 B–N5ch. wins.

| 11. B–B4! | Q–N3! |

Not 11 . . . , O–O?; 12 B×P!, etc.

12. B–QN3	B–QR3!
13. N–R4	Q–Q5!
14. Q×Q?	

This is the end of White's initiative. Much more promising is 14 Q–B3!, Q–K5; 15 Q×Q, P×Q; 16 KR–K1, P–Q4; 17 P–QB3, O–O; 18 B–N3 followed by N–B5 with strong pressure.

14.	B×Q
15. P–B4	O–O
16. QR–Q1	B–B3?

By playing 16 . . . , P–B4! Black maintains a splendid position. The inaccurate text allows White to develop in-

93

genious winning chances by sacrificing his Queen Bishop.

17. **KR–K1**   **P–N4!?**

Forcing the issue.

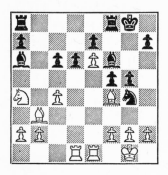

18. **B×QP!?**   **P×B**
19. **R×P**

Now White has a powerful attacking position and aside from the obvious 20 R×P he threatens 20 P–B5 with a view to 21 P–K7ch.

19.   **B–K4!**
20. **P–B5!**

Much stronger than 20 R× P, B–QN2 with counterplay for Black.

20.   **KR–K1!**

The acceptance of the second sacrifice is too dangerous, for example: 20 . . . , B×R; 21 P–K7ch., K–N2; 22 P×B, KR–K1; 23 P–Q7, QR–Q1?!; 24 P×R/K8(Q), R×Q; 25 P–B3, N–B3; 26 R–K6, with a won ending.

More complicated, but also unfavorable for Black is 20

. . . , B×Pch.; 21 K–R1, B×R; 22 P×B, N×Pch.; 23 K–N1, N–K5; 24 P–K7ch., K–N2; 25 P×R(Q)ch., R×Q; 26 P–Q7, R–Q1; 27 R×N!, P×R; 28 N–B5, K–B3; 29 N×B, R×P; 30 N–B5, and Black's King Pawn will go lost after White plays K–B2–K3, Black being unable to play 30 . . . , R–Q7.

21. **P–N3!**

Now the subtlety of Black's defense in choosing 19 . . . , B–K4! is clear.

If 21 P–KR3, B–R7ch.; 22 K–R1, B×R; 23 P×B, N× Pch.; 24 K–N1, N–K5; 25 P–K7ch., K–N2, and the Pawns are held.

21.   **B–B3!**

Still not 21 . . . , B×R; 22 P–K7ch., K–N2; 23 P×B, N–B3; 24 N–B5! (the move not available to White in the previous note), B–B1; 25 B–R4, and White's pressure is too powerful.

22. **R×P**

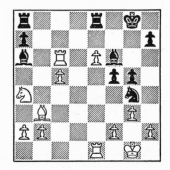

22.   B—QN2!

Insufficient would be 22 ... , B—N4?; 23 R—Q6, B—K4 (if 23 ... , B×N; 24 B×B, R—K2; 25 B—Q7); 24 P—KR3!, B×R; 25 P×B, N—B3; 26 N—B5, etc.

| 23. | R—B7 | B—K5 |
| 24. | N—B3 | B×N! |

If 24 ... , B—Q5?; 25 N×B, P×N; 26 R×KP, B×Pch.; 27 K—N2, N—B3; 28 R—QN4, B—K6; 29 R/N4—N7, and Black is helpless.

| 25. | P×B | N—K4 |

Black's defense has been so successful that the worst threats are over though the passed Pawns remain. He is now able to interpolate a little attack of his own.

26. R—Q1

Threatening to double Rooks on the seventh rank.

26.   N—B6ch.

But not 26 ... , KR—QB1?? (or 26 ... , QR—B1??); 27 R×Rch., R×R; 28 R—Q8ch.!, R×R; 29 P—K7ch., winning at once.

| 27. | K—B1 | N×Pch. |
| 28. | K—K1 | |

Of course not 28 K—K2?, B—B6ch.

28.		N—B6ch.
29.	K—K2	N—K4
30.	R/Q1—Q7!	

Recovering the Pawn, for if 30 ... , P—KR3; 31 R—N7ch., K—B1; 32 R—R7 still threatening mate. Black's defense still has to be extremely accurate.

30.		P—B5!
31.	R—N7ch.	K—R1
32.	R×NP	B—Q6ch.!

Now Black suddenly produces a threat to win the game himself. Of course White cannot reply 33 K—Q2 because of ... , N—B6ch.

33. K—Q1   P×P!

The point. White cannot play 34 R×N? because of 34 ... , P×P; 35 R—B7, R—KB1, winning.
Nor can White play 34 P—KB4? (to get another passed Pawn) because of 34 ... , R—KN1! and wins.

34.	P×P	N—N3
35.	R—Q5	B—K5
36.	R—Q6	B—B4

It begins to look as if White's proud King Pawn cannot last much longer.

| 37. | B—Q5 | QR—N1 |
| 38. | P—B6 | N—B1 |

If now 39 P—K7, N—N3; 40 B—B7, R×P; 41 B×N, B—N5ch.! followed by ... , R×R and wins. But Schlechter has a way out.

39. R—QN7!

Temporarily holding the King Pawn, for if now 39 ... , N×P?; 40 R×R wins.

Note, also, that the variation of the previous comment does not apply now that White's Rook at QN7 is protected.

39.		QR–B1
40.	P–K7	N–N3
41.	B–B7	R×KP
42.	B×N	B–N5ch.!

Although he has two pieces *en prise*, Black can save both of them owing to the position of White's King, and in fact this enables him to save the game. He now succeeds in remaining a piece ahead.

43.	K–B1	R–K8ch.
44.	K–N2	P×B
45.	R×NP	B–B4
46.	R–B6	B–K5
47.	R×P	R–N8ch.
48.	K–R3	B×P
	Drawn	

The culmination of a magnificently accurate defense. Both of White's advanced passed Pawns have fallen and Black now threatens . . . , B–N4 followed by . . . , R×P mate. White has nothing better than to take perpetual check.

GAME 27

Mieses—Capablanca

BERLIN, 1913

Jacques Mieses (born 1865) played in his first masters' tournament at Nuremberg, 1888, and what may be his last at Hastings, 1946. His style was extremely aggressive and he delighted in such risky gambits as the Danish. This brought him uneven results in tournaments, little success in matches, but frequent brilliancy prizes.

CENTER GAME

White	Black
Mieses	Capablanca

1.	P–K4	P–K4
2.	P–Q4	P×P
3.	Q×P	N–QB3
4.	Q–K3	N–B3
5.	N–QB3	B–N5
6.	B–Q2	O–O
7.	O–O–O	R–K1

By simple play against White's risky opening, Black has secured the win of a Pawn. If now 8 P–B3, P–Q4!

8.	Q–N3?!	N×P
9.	N×N	R×N
10.	B–KB4	Q–B3

Not liking 10 . . . , P–Q3, which allows White time for a promising attack.

If now 11 B×P?, P—Q3; 12 B×P, Q—R3ch.! 13 K—N1, Q—Q7! and wins.

11.	N—R3	P—Q3
12.	B—Q3	N—Q5!
13.	B—K3!	

Naturally not 13 B×R??, N—K7ch., winning the Queen.

Also, if 13 P—QB3, N—K7ch.; 14 B×N, R×B; 15 Q—Q3 (if 15 P×B??, Q×P mate), B×N! leaving White's Bishop unguarded.

13. **B—N5?**

Correct was 13 ... , R—N5!; 14 B×N, R×B; 15 P—QB3, B×P; 16 P×B, R—KN5; 17 Q—K3, Q×Pch.; 18 B—B2, Q×Qch.; 19 P×Q, R×P, with a winning game.

14. **N—N5!**

14 P—KB3 only gives equality after 14 ... , R×B; 15 Q×B.

If 14 P—QB3, B×P; 15 P×B, N—K7ch.; 16 B×N, Q×Pch.; 17 K—N1, R—N5 mate.

And finally if 14 B×N, R×B; 15 P—QB3, B×R; 16 R×B, R×B; 17 Q×R, B—B4, with a Pawn ahead. Black's combination is seen in all its ingenuity.

14. **R×B**

The only move.

If White now takes the Rook, Black plays ... , B×R and still comes out a Pawn ahead.

15. **Q×B!** **N—K7ch.**

By his last move, White has proved the whole combination to have been unsound after all.

Black must now lose the exchange, for if 15 ... , R—K2?; 16 B×Pch., K—B1; 17 R×N wins a piece.

| 16. | B×N | R×B |
| 17. | N—K4! | |

A tactical finesse, enabling him to capture on K4 instead of on K2. With the exchange ahead in this simplified position, any player might expect to win.

17.		R×N
18.	Q×R	Q—N4ch.
19.	P—B4	Q—N4
20.	P—B3	B—B4
21.	KR—K1	Q—B3
22.	R—Q5?	

An error of judgment. He cannot force the King side and get a quick mate by weight of material, so the logical course was 22 Q×Q, P×Q; 23

98   MIESES—CAPABLANCA

R–K7 with a winning end game.

22.   Q–Q2
23. P–B5

And here 23 Q–K7!, with the same idea, is better. Black cannot then reply 23 . . . , Q–N5?? because of 24 Q–K8ch.! leading to mate.

Now that White has wasted two moves, Black, whose position still does not appear to hold any promise, brings all his pieces to bear on White's King with an economy of moves that is quite remarkable.

23.   P–QB3
24. R–Q2   P–Q4
25. Q–B3?

There was no reason for the Queen to move. 25 P–KN4 is the logical move to furnish some justification for his 23rd move.

25.   B–K2!

Seizing his opportunity to post the Bishop on a much better diagonal. He also prevents 26 P–B6 and threatens 26 . . . , B–N4.

26. R/Q2–K2 B–B3

The Bishop is now trained on White's castled position.

27. Q–R5   P–KR3!
28. P–KN4   K–R2!

Concluding a deep maneuver. If now 29 P–KR4?? (to play 30 P–N5), Black

wins the Queen with 29 . . . , P–KN3!

29. K–N1   R–Q1

The first stage is completed. Black will soon proceed with the advance of his Queen-side Pawns.

30. R–Q1   P–B4
31. Q–R3   Q–R5!

The Black Queen is aggressively posted here.

32. R/K2–Q2   Q–K5ch.
33. K–R1   P–QN4!

Threatening . . . , P–N5. The way in which Black has seized the initiative is an object lesson in the correct use of material.

34. Q–N2   Q–R5!

If now 35 R×P?, Q×Rch.!, forcing mate.

35. K–N1   P–N5

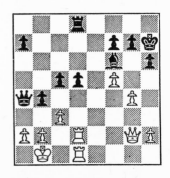

36. P×P?

The best defensive chance is 36 P–B4! forcing . . . , P–

Q5 and thus putting an end to the Bishop's pressure against White's QN2.

| 36. | Q×P |

Now 37 R×P is answered by 37 . . . , R×R; 38 R×R, B×P!, with a winning attack (39 Q×B, Q—K5ch., picking up the Rook with decisive advantage).

| 37. | P—QR3 | Q—R5 |
| 38. | R×P | R—QN1! |

Black has a winning attack, as he demonstrates very forcefully.

| 39. | R/Q5—Q2 | P—B5! |

Much stronger than 39 . . . , Q×RP.

| 40. | Q—N3 | R—N6 |
| 41. | Q—Q6 | P—B6 |

Another way is 41 . . . , B× P!; 42 R×B, P—B6!

| 42. | R—QB2 | P×P |
| 43. | R—Q3 | Q—K5! |

White has battled hard to stave off the attack and just when he seems to have succeeded, Black prevents 44 R× R by the threat of . . . , Q— K8ch. forcing mate.

44. R—Q1

A much harder win for Black is the elegant variation 44 R/B2—Q2, R—B6!; 45 R— Q1, B—N4!; 46 K×P, R—B3; 47 Q—Q5, R—N3ch., etc.

| 44. | | R—QB6! |

Resigns

For if 45 R—Q2, R×R; 46 R×R, Q—K8ch., forcing mate; and if 45 Q—Q2, R×P—the very move White has fought to prevent.

Black has not only escaped defeat but has actually won a lost game.

GAME 28

Capablanca—Marshall

RUY LOPEZ

White	Black
Capablanca	Marshall
1. P–K4	P–K4
2. N–KB3	N–QB3
3. B–N5	P–QR3
4. B–R4	N–B3
5. O–O	B–K2
6. R–K1	P–QN4
7. B–N3	O–O
8. P–B3	P–Q4!?

The Marshall Variation, in which a Pawn is sacrificed for a strong attack, was introduced to master play in this game.

9. P×P	N×P
10. N×P	N×N
11. R×N	N–B3
12. R–K1	

Subsequently, 12 P–Q4, B–Q3; 13 R–K2, was preferred as a defense, but Capablanca is out of the book and has to improvise. He said afterward that as soon as Marshall allowed him to play the Ruy Lopez, he suspected a prepared variation was coming, for Marshall had never faced a Ruy Lopez from Capablanca since his unhappy experience against it in the match of 1909. Capablanca anticipated that the attack would be "terrific."

12.	B–Q3
13. P–KR3	N–N5?!

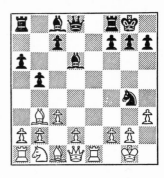

The attack begins and with it a period of intense crisis.

If in reply to the text move, White plays 14 P×N, then 14 . . . , Q–R5; 15 P–N3, B×P/N6; 16 P×B, Q×Pch.; 17 K–B1, B×P; 18 Q–B2 (if 18 R–K2, B–R6ch. forces mate), B–R6ch.; 19 K–K2, QR–K1ch., and mate follows.

The right way to repulse the attack is 14 P×N, Q–R5; 15 Q–B3!, Q–R7ch.; 16 K–B1, B×P; 17 Q×B, Q–R8ch.; 18 K–K2, QR–K1ch.; 19 B–K6!, R×Bch.; 20 Q×R!, Q–R4ch.; 21 P–N4!

14. Q–B3!	Q–R5
15. P–Q4!	N×P!
16. R–K2!	

If 16 Q×N, B–R7ch.! (16 . . . , B–N6?? allows the brilliant reply 17 Q×Pch.!!, R×Q; 18 R–K8 mate, showing how delicately the game is now balanced); 17 K–B1, B–N6; 18 Q–K2 (now if 18 Q×Pch.??, the Queen is captured with a check), B×P!; 19 P×B, QR–K1, and wins (for example 20 Q×R, Q×Pch.).

After the text, the attack must ease a little, as Black loses a piece.

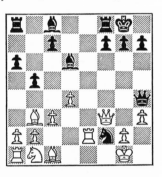

16.   **B–KN5?!**

The attack is continued with the utmost ferocity.

If instead 16 . . . , N×Pch.?; 17 P×N, B×P; 18 R–K4, etc.

Or 16 . . . , B×P; 17 P×B, N×Pch.; 18 K–B1, N–N4; 19 Q–N2, and in either case, White's attack is spent.

But 16 . . . , N–N5! keeps the attack alive. If then 17 R–K8! (not 17 P×N?, B×P winning), N–B3; 18 R×Rch., K×R; 19 N–Q2!, R–N1; 20 N–B1, B–N2, with fairly even prospects.

17.   **P×B**   **B–R7ch.**

On 17 . . . , N×P? White has 18 B–KB4!

18.   **K–B1**   **B–N6**
19.   **R×N**

White has fought his way into slightly calmer water. He obtains two pieces for the Rook, but is still behind in development.

19.   **Q–R8ch.**
20.   **K–K2**   **B×R**

Or 20 . . . , Q×B; 21 Q×B, Q×Pch.; 22 K–Q3, Q×R; 23 K–B2, and Black's initiative has petered out.

21.   **B–Q2**   **B–R5**
22.   **Q–R3**   **QR–K1ch.**
23.   **K–Q3**   **Q–B8ch.**
24.   **K–B2**   **B–B7**
25.   **Q–B3**   **Q–N8**

White's hardest task would come after 25 . . . , R–K7!; 26 N–R3!, R×Bch.; 27 K×R, Q×R; 28 Q×B, Q×Pch., etc.

26.   **B–Q5!**   **P–QB4**

A last attempt to revivify his flagging attack, but White is now poised for his counterthrust. The problem of Queenside development is to be solved by the advance of the Queen-side Pawns.

27.   **P×P**   **B×P**
28.   **P–N4**   **B–Q3**
29.   **P–R4**   **P–QR4**

Allows White a dangerous passed Pawn, but the collapse

of his attack is manifest in any event.

30.	RP×P	P×P
31.	R—R6	P×P
32.	N×P	B—N5
33.	P—N6!	B×N
34.	B×B	P—R3

The picture has now changed completely, and Black is helpless against the passed Pawn, for the moment his Rook leaves the first rank, his KB2 again become vulnerable.

35.	P—N7	R—K6

36. B×Pch.!

Forcing the Pawn home, for if in reply 36 . . . , K—R1; 37 R×P mate.

Or 36 . . . , K—R2; 37 Q—B5ch., K—R1; 38 R×P mate.

36.		R×B
37.	P—N8(Q)ch.	K—R2
38.	R×Pch.	Resigns

It is mate in two after 38 . . . , K×R (38 . . . , P×R; 39 Q×R mate); 39 Q—R8ch., K—N3 (or 39 . . . , K—N4); 40 Q—R5 mate.

GAME 29

Rubinstein—Alekhine

LONDON, 1922

Alexander Alekhine (1892–1946), Russian by birth and French by adoption, was world champion from 1927 to 1946, except for the period 1935–37. At his best, he was perhaps the most completely equipped and gifted chess player of all time, at home in open and close positions, orthodox and experimental, sound in theory and fiery in imagination. In his early years overshadowed by Lasker and Capablanca, he showed by his decisive victories in such tournaments as San Remo, 1930, and Bled, 1931, that in the fullness of maturity he was as great if not greater than they.

QUEEN'S GAMBIT DECLINED

	White	Black
	Rubinstein	Alekhine
1.	N–KB3	P–Q4
2.	P–Q4	N–KB3
3.	P–B4	P–B3
4.	N–B3	P×P
5.	P–QR4	B–B4
6.	P–K3	P–K3
7.	B×P	B–QN5
8.	O–O	O–O
9.	N–K2	

The theme of this opening is control of White's K4, and with the text move Rubinstein evolves an elaborate plan to get rid of Black's Queen Bishop. The more logical way to continue the fight for control of the center is 9 Q–K2.

From this point on, the battle for control of the vital square is fought out with all the intensity and persistence of which the players are capable.

9.		QN–Q2
10.	N–N3	B–N3
11.	N–R4	P–B4!

He exploits White's time-consuming maneuvers with the Knights to begin an energetic fight for the center.

12.	N×B	RP×N
13.	P×P	N×P
14.	Q–K2	KN–K5!

Preventing 15 P–K4.

15.	N×N	N×N
16.	Q–N4	N–B3
17.	Q–B3	Q–B2!

Gaining time to prevent P–K4.

18.	P–QN3	Q–K4
19.	R–R2	N–K5
20.	P–R5!?	

Preventing the reinforcement of the Bishop by . . . ,

104

P—R4 and making R—R4 possible in some cases. But the move is two-edged and cedes Black counterchances. 20 B—N2 is more straightforward.

| 20. | KR—Q1 |
| 21. B—N2 | B—B6 |

Not 21 . . . , Q—KB4; 22 R—R4, B—Q7; 23 B×KP, etc.

| 22. B×B | N×B |
| 23. R—B2 | |

White now threatens, by means of 24 KR—B1, N—Q4; 25 P—K4, to control the key squares and come out with the better game. But, thanks to White's 20th move, Black can maintain the Knight at his dominating post.

23.	P—QN4!
24. P×P e.p.	P×P
25. KR—B1	N—R7!
26. R—K1	P—QN4
27. B—B1	N—B6
28. Q—B4!	

If 28 P—K4, P—N5, and the first stage of the game ends in equality. White prefers a game that will allow him to use the open center files later.

28.	Q×Q
29. P×Q	P—N5
30. P—N3	R—R6

Alekhine calls this waste of time, recommending the immediate transfer of Black's King to the center.

| 31. B—B4 | K—B1 |
| 32. K—N2 | K—K2 |

33. R—K5!	R—QB1
34. R—Q2	R—Q1
35. R—B2	R—QB1
36. P—R4!?	

Rubinstein is not content with a draw by repetition.

| 36. | N—Q4 |

This leads to difficulties. 36 . . . , R—B3 would avoid all danger.

37. R/B2—K2!

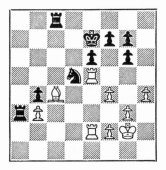

Now White has succeeded in developing a strong game in the center. The immediate threat is 38 R×N winning a piece.

| 37. | N—B6 |

If 37 . . . , N—N3?; 38 B× P!, P×B; 39 R×Pch., K—B2; 40 R×N, R×P; 41 R—N7ch., K—B3; 42 R/K2—K7, with advantage to White.

| 38. R—Q2 | R—B3 |
| 39. P—R5! | |

Trying to increase his pressure by an ingenious Pawn sacrifice, the primary object being to weaken Black's King Pawn. A new intensity comes into the game.

39.		P–B3
40.	R–K3	P×P
41.	P–B5	P–K4
42.	R/K3–Q3!	

Threatening mate in three moves. His initial plan foiled, White has switched to a different and even more menacing one—penetration into Black's position via the Queen file.

42.		R–R2
43.	R–Q8!?	

Again Rubinstein courageously spurns the draw, which he could have by 43 P–B3 (preventing . . . , N–K5), N–N8; 44 R/Q2–Q1, N–B6; 45 R/Q1–Q2, N–N8, etc.

43.		N–K5

He must prevent R–KN8.

44.	R/Q2–Q5!	R–Q3!

And not 44 . . . , N–Q3?; 45 R–KN8!, N×P; 46 R/Q5–Q8, N–Q3; 47 R–N8!, winning.

45.	R–KN8!	

Threatening to win the exchange, in the event that Black heedlessly plays 45 . . . , R×R?; 46 B×R, etc. In this apparently lost position, Alekhine finds a reply which neutralizes 46 R×NPch.

45.		R–R7!
46.	R×NPch.	K–B1

47.	R–N8ch.!	

Still neither player can tip the scales in his own favor. White must now adopt this very ingenious method either to force a draw or to get back to intercept the attack.

47.		K×R
48.	R–Q2ch.	K–N2
49.	R×R/R2	R–Q7!
50.	R×R	N×R
51.	B–Q5	

A drawn ending has been reached after all—but it is by no means easy to demonstrate.

51.		P–K5!

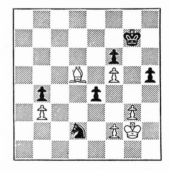

52.	P–B4??	

But this is fatal, for not only does it give Black a passed Pawn, it enables him to keep White's King out of action in a corner.

Much better is the line suggested by Burn: 52 P–N4!, P–R5 (if 52 . . . , K–R3; 53 K–N3, K–N4; 54 P–B4ch., P×P e.p.; 55 P×P, K×BP; 56 B–B7); 53 K–R3, N–B6;

54 P—N5 (if 54 B×P?, N—N4ch.), P×P; 55 B×P, N—Q7; 56 B—B2, K—B3; 57 K—N4, N—B8; 58 B—Q1, drawing.

52.		P—K6!
53.	K—N1	K—B1
54.	K—N2	K—K2
55.	B—N8	K—Q3
56.	B—B7	K—B4
57.	B×P	N×P

Allowing White to bring his King across at last, but now the Black King is also in range.

58.	K—B3	K—Q5
59.	B—B7	K—Q6!
60.	B×N	K—Q7
61.	B—B4	P—N6
62.	B×P	P—K7
	Resigns	

A fierce struggle that taxed the abilities of both of these great masters.

GAME 30

Reti—Becker

VIENNA, 1923

Richard Reti (1889–1929), a Czech, was one of the most original masters of the twentieth century and a leader of the school that revolted against the dogmas of Tarrasch and was dubbed "Hypermodern." The chief feature of their theory was that occupation of a center square or squares was often less effective and certainly less flexible than remote control. The excesses of the Hypermoderns soon faded, but their teachings left their mark and brought new vitality into a chess that was becoming too orthodox.

Albert Becker is a prominent Austrian master who has frequently figured in the prize list of continental tournaments.

ENGLISH OPENING
(in effect)

	White	*Black*
	Reti	Becker
1.	N—KB3	N—KB3
2.	P—B4	P—B4
3.	P—KN3	P—KN3
4.	B—N2	B—N2
5.	N—B3	N—B3
6.	P—Q3	O—O

In symmetrical positions, the player who first breaks the symmetry may acquire a lasting initiative, but he runs a risk in making the effort. In the present game the risk is great, and the effort is proportionately taxing. The result is an exciting game full of tense moments.

7. **B–K3**   **P–Q3**
8. **P–KR3**

Not yet 8 Q–Q2 (with a view to 9 B–R6) because of 8 . . . , N–KN5.

8.   **B–Q2**
9. **Q–Q2**   **R–N1**

Projecting an advance on the Queen Knight file, which ought to discourage White from castling Queen side—but it doesn't.

The alternative, leading to a totally different kind of game, is 9 . . . , R–K1, in order to answer B–R6 with . . . , B–R1!

10. **B–R6**   **N–K1**
11. **P–KR4!**

Indicating his intention of forsaking the positional basis of the opening and of going in for a combinative attack. The King Rook Pawn is to be given up to open the file for the Rook, but the whole idea is somewhat speculative and difficult to appraise.

11.   **B–N5!**
12. **P–R5!**   **PXP**

On 12 . . . , BXP White gets a dangerous attack by 13 BXB, NXB; 14 P–KN4!, BXP; 15 Q–R6, P–B3!; 16 QXPch., K–B2; 17 N–R4, etc.

13. **N–KR4**   **Q–Q2**
14. **B–K4**   **N–Q5!**

Threatening to break up White's attack completely by

15 . . . , N–B7ch.; 16 QXN, BXB.

15. **O–O–O!**

The center is getting too uncomfortable for White's King. Note the wild variation 15 P–B3, P–B4; 16 B–Q5ch., P–K3—a position virtually beyond analysis.

15.   **P–N4!**

Beginning a sharp counter-attack that will test White's resources to the utmost.

16. **P–B3!**   **P–N5!**

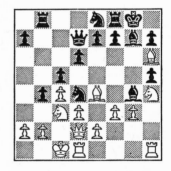

Black has now developed his own attack, and White appears to be in difficulties.

Thus if 17 N–Q5, NXPch.!; 18 K–N1 (on 18 K–B2, Q–R5ch. is decisive, or if 18 QX N, BXBch., etc.), N–B6ch.; 19 NXN, PXN; 20 Q–N5, RX Pch., followed by . . . , Q–R5.

Or if 17 PXB, PXN; 18 PX BP, Q–R5!; 19 QR–N1, Q–R6ch.; 20 K–Q1, R–N8ch. with crushing effect.

Another possibility is 17 PX

B, P×N; 18 Q—N5, N×Pch.;
19 K—N1, R×Pch.; 20 K—R1,
R×Pch.!; 21 K×R, Q—R5ch.;
22 K—N1, P—B7 mate.

17. **N—N5!**

A brilliant idea. If now 17
. . . , N×N; 18 P×N, B—K3;
19 B—B6 followed by 20 Q—
N5 with a winning game.

Or 17 . . . , B—K3; 18 N×N,
P×N; 19 P—N4! and White's
attack rolls on while Black's is
at a standstill.

17.   **N×Pch.!**

A fine move, for if in reply
18 Q×N, B×Bch., and Black
is two Pawns ahead with a
comfortable game; while if 18
K—N1, N—B6ch.!; 19 P×N,
P×P and wins.

White must therefore allow
Black to sacrifice his Knight
for the complete disruption of
the White Pawns.

18. **K—B2!**   **N×P**

An interesting alternative is
18 . . . , B—K3, so that after
19 B×B, N×B; 20 Q×N, Black
can regain the lost piece with
20 . . . , P—B4 or 20 . . . ,
P—QR3.

19. **P×B**   **N×B**

An amusing variation is 19
. . . , N×R; 20 R×N, Q×P??;
21 B—B5, Q—N6; 22 B—B4,
and the Queen is trapped!

Or 19 . . . , N×R; 20 R×N,
P—R3; 21 N—B5! with a win-
ning attack, for example 21
. . . , P—K3; 22 N×B, N×N;

23 N×P!, Q×N; 24 Q—N5
forcing mate.

20. **P×N**   **Q—K3!**

Again . . . , P—R3 can be
answered by N—B5.

The text move leaves White
in a terrible position, faced
as he is with a threat to his
Bishop, threats to three Pawns
(in two cases with check),
and after the fall of the Queen
Bishop Pawn, with a threat to
the Knight. He has to stake
everything on his attack on
Black's King.

21. **N—B5!**   **Q×BPch.**
22. **K—N1**   **Q×KPch.**
23. **K—R1**

Black has secured the re-
markable and very unusual
bargain of six Pawns for a
minor piece.

23.   **P×P?!**

If 23 . . . , Q×P?; 24 N×B,
N×N; 25 QR—N1 and wins.

Or 23 . . . , R×N; 24 Q—
N5, Q—K4; 25 B×B, N×B; 26
QR—K1, Q—B3; 27 N×Pch.,
winning.

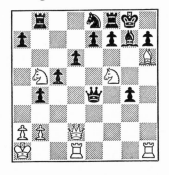

24. B×B?

But here Reti, after much ingenious play, goes wrong. The winning move, according to Becker, was 24 Q—N5!:

a) 24 . . . , Q—K4; 25 B×B, N×B; 26 N×Pch., K—R1; 27 R×Pch.!, followed by mate.

b) 24 . . . , P—B3; 25 Q—R5, R×N; 26 B×B, N×B; 27 Q×Pch., K—B2; 28 Q×Nch., K—K1; 29 KR—K1, and wins.

24.   N×B

After 24 . . . , Q×N; 25 B×R, R×N; 26 B×P, White with a Rook for five somewhat loose Pawns is better off.

25. N×N

25 N—N3 looks stronger, but Black can fight back: 25 . . . , Q—K4; 26 Q—R6, P—B3!, etc.

25.   K×N
26. Q—R6ch.   K—N1??

A time-pressure blunder. After 26 . . . , K—R1! White has to fight for the draw.

27. QR—KN1!

With the terrible threat of 28 R×Pch.!

27.   K—R1

Too late; however, if 27 . . . , KR—B1; 28 R—R4!, P—B4; 29 Q×Pch., K—B1; 30 Q—N6!, etc.

28. R×P

The first Pawn loss Black suffers is fatal for him. As curious and remarkable a game as any ever played.

28.   Q×Rch.
29. Q×Q   R—N1

Or 29 . . . , R×N; 30 R—R4, etc.

30. R×Rch.   Resigns

GAME 31

Znosko-Borovsky—Alekhine

PARIS, 1925

Eugene Znosko-Borovsky (born 1884), a prominent Russian master in the years before the First World War, is best known for his lively and excellent treatises on various phases of the game and is perhaps the greatest teacher of elementary chess of all time.

ALEKHINE'S DEFENSE

White	Black
Znosko-Borovsky	Alekhine
1. P–K4	N–KB3
2. P–K5	N–Q4
3. P–QB4	N–N3
4. P–Q4	P–Q3
5. P–B4	

Tartakover has well said that in this opening White has his initiative to defend. The method adopted here by White is the most enterprising and also the most dangerous.

5.	PXP
6. BPXP	N–B3
7. B–K3	B–B4
8. N–KB3	P–K3
9. N–B3	N–N5
10. R–B1	P–B4

An attempt to undermine White's center, now that the Pawns have been "enticed" forward.

11. P–QR3	PXP
12. B–N5?!	

No doubt hoping for 12

..., B–K2; 13 BXB, QXB; 14 N–QN5, N–B3; 15 N–Q6ch., with a good game; though after 12 . . . , Q–Q2, he can achieve little, and the simple 12 NXP was sounder.

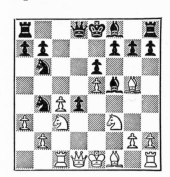

| 12. | PXN! |

A startling reply indicating that he is going all out to win.

| 13. BXQ | RXB?! |

Alekhine later pointed out that the proper move was 13 . . . , PXP!:

a) 14 BXN (if 14 PXN, RXB wins), PXR(Q); 15 QX

Q, N—B7ch.; 16 K—B2, P×B,
with a winning game.

b) 14 B—N5!, P×R(Q); 15
B×Q, N—B7ch.; 16 K—B2, R—
Q1; 17 Q—K2, B—B4ch.; 18
K—N3, O—O, with material
and positional advantage.

14.	Q—N3!	P×P
15.	Q×P	N—R5
16.	Q—R1!	N—B7ch.
17.	R×N	B×R
18.	N—Q4!	

Much stronger than 18 B—
K2 (against . . . , R—Q8ch.),
B—QB4!, and White is virtu-
ally without moves.

18.		B—N3
19.	P—B5!	

The point. He now develops
his Bishop with good effect
through the threat of B—N5ch.
winning a piece.

19.		N×P
20.	B—N5ch.	N—Q2
21.	Q—B3!	

White finds the best tactical
chance every time.

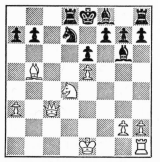

21.		P—QR3?

Pressed for time, Alekhine
throws away his last winning
chances. He can gain a decisive tempo with 21 . . . , B—
K2!; 22 Q—B7, P—QR3; 23
B—R4, B—K5!; 24 O—O, P—
QN4; 25 B—B2, B—QB4, re-
pulsing the attack without any
trouble.

22.	B×Nch.	R×B
23.	Q—B8ch.!	

Preparing to give up a piece
to keep Black tied up.

If 23 O—O, Black has a
choice of 23 . . . , B×P; 24
Q×B, R×N, or 23 . . . , P—N3,
threatening . . . , R×N!

Or if 23 N—B3, B—Q6; 24
Q—B8ch., R—Q1; 25 Q×P, B×
P; 26 Q—B6ch., K—K2, and
Black obtains a quick deploy-
ment of his pieces.

23.		R—Q1
24.	Q×P!	R×N
25.	Q—B6ch.	R—Q2
26.	O—O!	B—Q6!?

26 . . . , K—K2 forces White
to take an immediate per-
petual check. But Alekhine
wants to induce his opponent
to plunge into further complications.

| 27. | R×P!? | |

White also spurns the im-
mediate draw by 27 Q—B8ch.,
etc.

27.		B—B4ch.!
28.	K—R1	B—N4!
29.	Q×Pch.	R—K2!

Not 29 . . . , B—K2?; 30 R×Bch.!, etc.

Likewise after 29 . . . , K—Q1?; 30 R×Rch., B×R; 31 Q—Q5! White wins a piece.

30.	R×Rch.	B×R
31.	Q—B8ch.	B—Q1
32.	Q—K6ch.	B—K2

The simplest. If 32 . . . ,

K—B1; 33 P—QR4!, B×P; 34 Q—B5ch., K—K1; 35 Q—K6ch., and draws—but not 34 . . . , K—K2?; 35 Q—N4!, R—KB1; 36 Q—N4ch.!, winning.

| 33. | Q—B8ch. | B—Q1 |
| 34. | Q—K6ch. | Drawn |

A spirited game, full of subtle tactical points.

GAME 32

Tartakover—Bogolyubov

LONDON, 1927

Saviclly Tartakover, born 1887 in Russia later took French citizenship. An original and aggressive player, he always seeks to escape from the book, and this has perhaps cost him a number of prizes. He has, however, won many tournaments, as for example at Vienna, 1923; Liége, 1930; and at Hastings, 1946.

Ewfim D. Bogolyubov (born 1889), also a Russian by birth, was interned in Germany during the First World War and became a permanent resident in 1926. He rapidly achieved prominence in the 1920's, and his vigorous and aggressive style won him a number of tournaments, notably Moscow, 1925. By 1929 he was regarded as a challenger for the world title, but was soundly defeated twice, in 1929 and 1934, by Alekhine.

PONZIANI OPENING

	White	Black
	Tartakover	Bogolyubov
1.	P—K4	P—K4
2.	N—KB3	N—QB3
3.	P—B3	

Tartakover is fond of old and discarded openings.

| 3. | | N—B3 |
| 4. | P—Q4 | P—Q4 |

| 5. | KP×P | Q×P |
| 6. | B—K2 | P—K5!? |

Simpler is 6 . . . , P×P transposing into the Danish Gambit Declined. But Bogolyubov despises simpler lines.

| 7. | KN—Q2 | P—K6!? |

A sharp move, putting a keen edge on the game. It

cedes White an impressive Pawn center at the cost of a broken-up King side.

8.	P×P	Q×NP
9.	B—B3	Q—R6
10.	Q—K2	N—KN5

Preventing White from castling, as the exchange 11 B×N, B×B, is even less attractive for White.

11.	N—K4	Q—R5ch.
12.	K—Q1!	

If 12 N—N3, B—Q3; 13 Q—N2, N×RP, with advantage; and similarly, after 12 N—B2, N×RP, the resulting complications are not unfavorable for Black.

12.		B—Q2

The alternative was 12 . . . , P—B4, and if 13 B×N, P×N, with a position difficult to appraise.

13.	B—Q2!	O—O—O
14.	B—K1	Q—K2
15.	B×N	Q×N
16.	B—B3	Q—N3
17.	N—Q2	P—B3!

Another difficult decision. 17 . . . , P—B4 exerts more immediate effect in the center, but with the proviso that White may be able to open up the position later on by P—K4, giving his Bishops considerable scope.

The text move has a two-fold purpose: it guards Black from the worst effects of the possible advance P—K4—K5;

and it prepares a wholesale advance of Black's King-side Pawns.

18.	B—N3	P—KR4!
19.	KR—N1	P—R5
20.	B—B2	Q—B2
21.	P—K4	B—Q3
22.	B—K3	N—R4

Temporarily preventing N—B4—or permitting it only on the condition that White weakens his formation somewhat.

23.	P—N4	B—R5ch.
24.	K—K1	

The King's position is now not without danger. 24 K—B1 is safer.

24.		N—B3
25.	N—B4	

Threatens 26 N—N2.

25.		B×RP!

A counterattack just in time, for if 25 . . . , N—K2 (directed against 26 N—N2); 26 P—N5!, B×NP?; 27 N×Bch., wins a piece.

26. **N—N2!**

26 R—N2 is inadequate because of . . . , B—N6ch. But after Tartakover's last move, both Bishops are *en prise*.

26.	**B×R**
27. **B×B**	**N×QP!**

He must lose another piece, for if 27 . . . , P—QN4; 28 N×B, P×N; 29 Q—R6ch., K—Q2; 30 B—N4ch., and White will have two Bishops for Rook and Pawn, with Black's game completely disorganized.

Attack and counterattack now continue at a fast pace.

28. **P×N**   **B—B3**

Preparing for another sacrifice, as 28 . . . , B—Q2; 29 R—B1, followed by 30 B—R2, leaves White with a powerful attack.

29. **P—Q5**	**B×P!**
30. **P×B**	**KR—K1!**

Black mobilizes the counterattack with wonted energy. With Rook and three connected passed Pawns against three minor pieces, he has arrived at a position that is exceedingly difficult to appraise.

31. **B—K3**   **P—KB4**

31 . . . , R×B will not do because of 32 Q×R, R—K1; 33 B—N4ch., P—B4; 34 B×Pch.!, etc.

32. **K—B1!**   **P—KN4!**

And not 32 . . . , P—B5, because of 33 B—N4ch. and 34 B—K6.

33. **Q—KB2**	**P—N5**
34. **B—R1!**	

If 34 B×NP, R×B!, with good prospects.

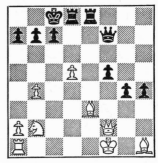

34.   **R×P?**

Continuing with characteristic boldness, but after 34 . . . , P—B5! White can hardly hope to win. If White declines the Bishop Pawn, the passed Pawns become too strong. However, if 35 Q×P (or 35 B×P, R—B1), Q×Qch.; 36 B×Q, R—B1 and Black should hold the ending.

35. **B—B4!**

After 35 B×R, Q×B, Black would threaten 36 . . . , P—N6; 37 Q—Q2, Q—R8ch.; 38 K—K2 (if 38 B—N1, Q—B6ch.), Q×R.

The reply 36 B—B4 allows 36 . . . , P—N6; 37 Q—N2, Q—N4ch.; 38 K—N1, R—K7, winning the Knight.

And if 36 Q—B4?, Q—R8ch.;

37 B—N1, Q—R6ch.; 38 K—B2, P—N6ch.; 39 K—B3, Q—R8 mate.

35.	R—K5!

Thrill follows thrill now that Black is committed to an all-out effort. He must close one of the two Bishops' diagonals, for a quiet move such as 35 . . . , R/Q4—Q1 allows 36 Q×QRP with a devastating attack.

36.	B×R!	P×B
37.	K—N1!	P—N6!

Black realizes that 37 . . . , R—KB4 loses quickly: 38 Q× QRP!, R×B; 39 R—Q1, P—B3; 40 Q—R8ch., K—B2; 41 Q—Q8 mate.

38.	Q—K3	Q—B3!
39.	R—N1	R—KB4
40.	Q×RP!	R—Q4

Tardily realizing that after 40 . . . , R×B; 41 Q—R8ch.!, K—Q2; 42 R—Q1ch., his game would be lost.

41.	Q—R8ch.	K—Q2
42.	Q×P	Q—Q5ch.
43.	K—R1	P—K6!

The seemingly dangerous 43 . . . , Q—B7 is answered by 44 Q×Rch., K—B1; 45 Q—B5ch.!, K—N2 (other King moves allow 46 B×Pch., exchanging Queens); 46 Q×Pch., followed by 47 Q—N2.

44.	R—QB1?

A time-pressure mistake. The right way was 44 Q× Pch.!, K—K3; 45 R—QB1!, and Black has no defense against the coming R—B6ch.

44.	P—N7ch.!

And not 44 . . . , Q—K5ch.; 45 K—N1, R—Q8ch., because White captures the Rook *with check*!

45.	K×P!

Not 45 K—N1, P—K7ch.; 46 K×P, Q—K5ch., and Black wins!

45.	P—R6ch.?

Missing his opportunity.

After 45 . . . , Q—K5ch.!; 46 K—N1, R—N4ch.; 47 B×R, Q×Q; 48 B×RP, Q×P; 49 N—B4, P—K7, Black has very good chances.

Out of the question for White, after 45 . . . , Q—K5ch.!, would be 46 K—R3?, Q—B6ch.; 47 K×P, R—R4 mate, or 46 K—B1, Q×Bch.; 47 K—N1, Q—N6ch.; 48 K—R1, Q—R6ch.; 49 K—N1, R—N4ch., and mate next move.

46.	K—B3!	K—K3
47.	R×P	P—R7
48.	Q—B6ch.	R—Q3

Or 48 . . . , K—B4; 49 R—B7ch. etc.

49.	Q—K8ch.	Resigns

For if 49 . . . , K—Q4 (or 49 . . . , K—B4); 50 Q—R5ch., K—K3; 51 Q—B7 mate. A titanic struggle from start to finish.

Capablanca—Nimzovich

BAD KISSINGEN, 1928

Aron Nimzovich (1886–1935), a Russian who adopted Denmark as his second country, first came into prominence early in the twentieth century. His style was so original that he has generally been regarded as the founder of the Hypermodern school; he was not only an iconoclast, but a great teacher as well. He was always highly placed in tournaments, his best result being the first prize at Carlsbad, 1929. However, he never obtained the match for the world title to which he was generally regarded as entitled.

NIMZOINDIAN DEFENSE

White	Black
Capablanca	Nimzovich
1. P–Q4	N–KB3
2. P–QB4	P–K3
3. N–QB3	B–N5
4. Q–B2	P–Q4
5. B–N5?	

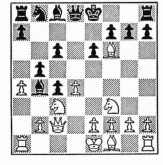

A move proved inferior for the first time in this game. Black's play, holding the gambit Pawn, leads to a great battle.

5 P×P is generally played here to avoid the complications that follow in the text.

5.	P×P!
6. N–B3	P–N4
7. P–QR4	P–B3
8. B×N!?	

Not 8 P–K3 because he hopes to take advantage of Black's weakness on the long diagonal.

8.   P×B

He dismisses 8 . . . , Q×B!! because of 9 P×P, P×P; 10 Q–K4, etc. Amazingly enough, this variation is quite playable for Black: 10 . . . , Q–N3!!; 11 Q×R, Q–B7!:

a) 12 Q×N, O–O!; 13 N–Q2, Q×P; 14 QR–N1, Q×N/B6, or 14 Q×RP, B×N; 15 R–Q1, B×P; 16 Q–B7, P–B6, and Black wins in either case.

b) 12 Q×P, Q×P; 13 R–Q1, B×Nch.; 14 N–Q2, B×

Nch.; 15 R×B, Q—N8ch.; 16
R—Q1, Q—N5ch.; 17 R—Q2,
P—B6!; 18 Q×N, O—O!; 19
Q—B7 (if 19 P—K3, P—B7!, or
19 K—Q1??, Q—N8 mate), Q—
N8ch.; 20 R—Q1, P—B7!

9.	P—KN3	P—QR3

Beginning an unexpected
maneuver, as a result of which
White's Bishop on the long
diagonal will bite on thin air.

10.	B—N2	R—R2
11.	O—O	R—Q2
12.	Q—B1	O—O
13.	Q—R6	B×N

The alternative answer to
the threat of N—K4 fails by
13 . . . , K—R1; 14 N—K4,
B—K2; 15 N/B3—N5!, P×N;
16 N—B6!, B×N; 17 B—K4,
forcing mate.

The text move frees White's
remaining Knight from the
defense of the Queen Pawn,
but it remains without much
future even so. On the other
hand, the exchange of Black's
good Bishop implies a weakening of the black squares in
Black's camp.

14.	P×B	K—R1
15.	N—Q2	P—KB4
16.	KR—N1	

If now 16 P—K4, P—K4, and
White's center goes to pieces
after 17 KP×P, R—Q3; 18 Q—
K3, KP×P; 19 BP×P, R×P;
20 N—B3, R—Q6.

White's last move threatens
17 N×P.

16.		P—K4!

On 16 . . . , B—N2 Tar-
takover gives 17 P×P, RP×P
(17 . . . , BP×P; 18 B×B, R×
B; 19 N×P favors White); 18
R—R7, and White stands well.

After 16 . . . , R—N2 Tartakover indicates a curious
drawing line: 17 N×P!, P×N;
18 R×R, B×R; 19 R—N1, B—
R1; 20 R×N!, Q×R; 21 Q—
B6ch., etc.

17.	N—B3

Changing his mind. There
seems to be more fight in 17
N×P, KP×P; 18 N—K5, R—
Q3; 19 Q—B1, QP×P; 20 Q×P,
Q—B3.

17.		R—Q3!
18.	Q—K3	

He must try and hold what
center he has, for if 18 Q—R5,
KP×P; 19 N—N5, P—R3; 20
N×Pch., R×N; 21 Q×R, QP×
P, and the Black Pawns will
win.

18.		P—K5
19.	N—Q2	N—Q2
20.	P—N4?!	

A fighting reply. A less
aggressive line would lead to
slow suffocation. Now the
game becomes very critical.

20.		N—B3
21.	NP×P	B×P?

The natural move and good
enough; but more decisive is
21 . . . , N—Q4!; 22 Q—R3 (if

22 Q×P?, N×P, or 22 Q—N3, R—N1), N—B5; 23 Q—K3, Q—N4; 24 Q×P (forced), R—N1, and wins.

22. **Q—B4**   **Q—Q2**
23. **B×P**

The only way to get freedom in the center, for if 23 N×KP, B×N; 24 B×B, R—N1ch.; 25 B—N2 (on King moves, 25 . . . , R—N5 is decisive), N—Q4; 23 Q—K5ch. (if 23 Q—B3, R/Q3—N3), P—B3; 27 Q—R5, N—B5, winning.

23.   **N×B**
24. **N×N**   **R—N3ch.**
25. **N—N3**

The climax of Black's play, for White must now lose the exchange.

If instead 25 K—B1, R—K1; 26 P—B3, B×N; 27 P×B, Q—R6ch., and wins. Or 25 K—R1, Q—Q4; 26 P—B3, R—K1, with the threat of 27 . . . , R×N; 28 P×R, B×Pch., forcing mate.

25.   **B×R**
26. **R×B**   **P—KB4**

Threatening 27 . . . , R—N5 followed by 28 . . . , P—B5.

27. **P—B3**   **Q—KN2?**

But now Black begins to go wrong, curiously enough in the same way as Mieses did against Capablanca in Game 27, by not forcing exchanges after obtaining a material advantage. More forcing was 27 . . . , Q—Q3; 28 Q×Q, R×Q;

29 P—K4, P×P; 30 P×P, R—B6.

28. **K—B2**   **Q—B3**
29. **P×P**   **BP×P**

Though Black's Queen-side Pawns look strong, White now has a passed Pawn that enables him to fight back with magnificent virtuosity.

However, if 29 . . . , RP×P; 30 P—Q5! breaks up Black's Pawns.

30. **R—Q1**   **K—N1?**

Once more . . . , Q—Q3! was the move. After the text move, Black must contend with considerable difficulties.

31. **P—Q5!**   **Q×P?**

The final misjudgment. 31 . . . , Q—Q3! was in order, with the following continuation indicated by Tartakover: 32 Q×Q, R×Q; 33 P—K4, P×P; 34 N×P, R—R3!; 35 P—Q6, K—B2, and wins.

32. **P—Q6**   **Q—B3**
33. **P—Q7**   **P—B6**
34. **N×P!**

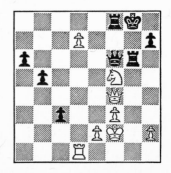

34.   P—B7!

Of course not 34 . . . , Q×N?; 35 Q×Q, R×Q; 36 P—Q8(Q)ch., and wins—likewise after 34 . . . , R—N4?; 35 R—Q5! (if 35 N—R6ch.?, Q×N!), R×N; 36 R×R, Q—N3ch.; 37 K—N2, R×R; 38 Q×R.

35.   R—Q6!

A big surprise.

35.   Q—Q1

Threatening . . . , R×R and still anticipating a won game. Other lines lead only to a probable draw, for example:
 a) 35 . . . , Q×R; 36 N×Q, R×Q; 37 P—Q8(Q)ch., R—B1; 38 Q—B7, R×N; 39 Q×P.
 b) 35 . . . , P—B8(Q); 36 Q×Q, Q×N; 37 P—Q8(Q), R×Q; 38 R×R/Q8ch.

White uses his passed Pawn with magnificent effect, so that Black's move is the only reasonable one.

36. Q—K5!!   R×N

Of course not 36 . . . , P—B8(Q)??; 37 R×Rch., P×R; 38 Q—N7 mate.
 On 36 . . . , R—N7ch.; 37 K×R, Q—N4ch.; 38 K—B2, P—B8(Q) White has a draw by 39 Q—Q5ch.! etc.

37. Q—K8ch.!

A final point—37 Q×R? loses.

37.   R—B1

If 37 . . . , K—N2; 38 R×Rch., P×R; 39 Q×Q, P—B8(Q); 40 Q—K7ch., K—R3; 41 P—Q8(Q), and White actually wins, so Black must submit to the draw by perpetual check.

38. R×Rch.   Drawn

Euwe—Bogolyubov

MATCH, 1928

Dr. Max Euwe (born 1901), the Dutch master, won the world championship from Alekhine in 1935, only to lose it again two years later. A player of deep and accurate positional sense, he has repeatedly won prizes in master tournaments, though often just failing to win the first prize.

QUEEN'S GAMBIT
DECLINED

White	Black
Euwe	Bogolyubov
1. P—Q4	P—Q4
2. P—QB4	P—K3
3. N—QB3	N—KB3
4. B—N5	QN—Q2
5. P—K3	P—B3
6. P—QR3	

Preventing the Cambridge Springs Defense.

6.	B—K2
7. N—B3	N—K5
8. B×B	Q×B
9. Q—B2	P—KB4

A solid variation in which, however, he will labor under the permanent disadvantage of weak black squares and a confined Bishop.

10. B—K2	O—O
11. O—O	R—B3

The freeing move . . . , P—K4 is impossible because of the loss of the Queen Pawn, and if first 11 . . . , N×N; 12 Q×N and . . . , P—K4 is still prevented.

12. N—K5!?

A double-edged move. He permanently prevents . . . , P—K4 but has to allow some weakening of his position on the King side. The more orthodox play is to operate on the Queen side by P—B5 and then P—QN4—5.

12.	QN×N
13. P×N	R—R3
14. P—KN3	

To prevent . . . , Q—R5. If he permits . . . , Q—R5 and then plays P—R3, Black can at once continue with . . . , P—KN4—5.

14.	B—Q2
15. P—B3	

[*See diagram in next column.*]

15. N×P!?

A bold sacrifice designed to take advantage of the weakness White has created. But probably the quieter line 15 . . . , N—N4 would in the end prove more effective.

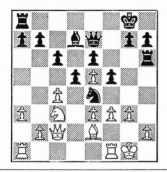

| 16. | PxN | Q–N4 |
| 17. | K–N2 | |

If 17 K–B2, R–R7ch.; 18 K–K1, QxKP; 19 P–B4, Qx Pch., with a good attack for the piece.

17.		R–N3
18.	P–KN4	QxP
19.	P–B4	BPxP

To prevent 20 P–N5 and 21 B–R5.

| 20. | Q–Q3 | Q–N3 |
| 21. | P–N4 | |

Preparing for 22 R–R1 with the threat of 23 RxP!, KxR; 24 R–R1ch., K–N1; 25 QxR, but later he chooses a different course. White is now beginning to recover the initiative.

21.		R–KB1
22.	P–QB5	Q–Q1
23.	Q–N3	P–KR4
24.	R–R1	R–R3
25.	QR–KB1	P–QN3

Black is entirely without prospects unless he can open some more lines.

26.	Q–R4	Q–R1
27.	B–Q3	P–R4
28.	Q–N5	B–K1

If 28 . . . , RPxP; 29 RxP, RxR; 30 QxR, R–B1 (directed against 31 B–R7ch.); 31 RPxP, with a great advantage.

29. R–R1

Black's maneuver has succeeded in making White halt his attack. If 29 N–R4, RPxP; 30 NxP, QxP, with good chances.

29.   Q–N1

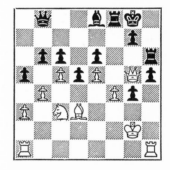

30. NPxP

This fails to keep Black contained. It was based on the line 30 . . . , PxRP; 31 QR–QN1, Q–R2; 32 N–R4 (not 32 R–N6, P–QR5), and Black cannot get out.

Better is 30 KR–QN1 (not 30 QR–QN1, RPxP; 31 RPx P, PxP; 32 PxP, Q–R2), Q–R2; 31 N–R4, P–N4; 32 N–B3 and White holds the Queen side.

30.		P—N4
31.	N—K2	Q—R2
32.	N—N3	

He cannot prevent Black's Queen from coming into the game, for if 32 KR—QB1, Q× RP, threatening . . . , Q—Q7.

32.		QXBP
33.	P—B5!	P—R5!
34.	R×P	

A most critical position, with both players on the attack.

Probably best is simply 34 N—K2, P—Q5; 35 N—B4, Q— B6; 36 P—B6, Q—Q7ch.; 37 K—B1, R—B2; 38 Q×NP, P— B4. The text move, which

looks strong, has one small flaw.

34.		R×R
35.	P—B6	

If 35 Q×R, Q—K6; 36 Q×P, Q×B; 37 P—B6, Q—N3, and Black can hold the position.

35.		R—R7ch.!

Resolving the problem by force.

36.	K×R	Q—KB7ch.
	Drawn	

After 37 K—R1, Q—B6ch.; White must play 38 K—R2, Q—B7ch., etc.—not 38 K—N1?, Q×Nch.; 39 K—B1, Q×Bch.; 40 K—K1, Q—R2, and wins. A keen-edged battle.

Vidmar–Euwe

CARLSBAD, 1929

Dr. Milan Vidmar (born 1885), of Yugoslav nationality, came into prominence early in the twentieth century, and for forty years has been a consistent prizewinner in master tournaments, though seldom taking a first prize. His victory at Bad Sliac, 1932, was one of his best achievements.

KING'S INDIAN
DEFENSE

White	Black
Vidmar	Euwe
1. P–Q4	N–KB3
2. N–KB3	P–KN3
3. B–N5	

An unorthodox development of the Bishop that almost inevitably leads to giving up the Bishop for the Knight.

3.	B–N2
4. QN–Q2	P–B4
5. P–K3	

He advances the Pawn only one square in order to set up a solid center in the hope of neutralizing Black's fianchettoed Bishop.

5.	P–N3
6. B–Q3	B–N2
7. O–O	P–KR3
8. B–KB4	P–Q3
9. P–B3	N–R4
10. Q–N3	

White allows a certain amount of disruption in his Pawn position to obtain new lines for his pieces. The safe

10 B–N3, N×B; 11 RP×N, offers fewer possibilities. As White plays, however, he ends up with an isolated Queen Pawn, leaving Black's King Bishop with ample striking power. Thus the idea of his 5th move is negated.

10.	N×B
11. P×N	O–O!

If 11 . . . , P×P; 12 N×P, and Black can give White an isolated Queen Pawn only at the cost of parting with his valuable King Bishop.

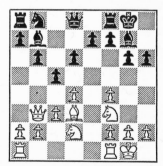

White can play to win a Pawn by 12 B×P, but after 12 . . . , P–B5!; 13 N×P (if 13

Q×BP?, P—Q4), P—Q4; 14 N/B4—K5, P×B; 15 N×P, R—B3, the position is very unclear.

Unsatisfactory for White is 12 P×P, QP×P; 13 B×P, B—Q4; 14 P—B4, B×N; 15 Q×B, P×B; 16 Q×R, Q×N, etc.

| *12.* | QR—Q1 | N—B3 |

Now B×P? is quite out of the question because of . . . , N—R4.

| *13.* | B—N1 | P×P |
| *14.* | P×P | |

He reconciles himself to the isolated Pawn because he wants to retain a strong grip on the center.

| *14.* | | P—K3 |

This weakens the Queen Pawn, but 14 . . . , N×P would not do because of 15 N×N, B×N; 16 B×P, KB×P; 17 B—N1, and Black's King side is permanently weak.

| *15.* | N—K4 | N—K2 |

15 . . . , P—Q4 would subsequently allow White to post a Knight powerfully at K5.

| *16.* | Q—R3! | N—B4 |
| *17.* | R—Q2 | |

Not 17 P—KN4?, N—R5!, and White has irretrievably weakened his castled position.

| *17.* | | Q—K2 |
| *18.* | N—N3 | N×N |

The immediate 18 . . . , KR—B1 was even better.

| *19.* | BP×N | KR—B1 |
| *20.* | P—KN4 | |

Black's exchange at move 18 has straightened out White's King-side Pawns and given him some attacking chances.

20.		R—B2
21.	P—B5	KP×P
22.	P×P	P—KN4
23.	R—K1	Q—B3

The immediate disruption of his King-side Pawns has been averted, and he threatens . . . , P—N5 winning the Knight.

| *24.* | P—R3 | QR—QB1 |
| *25.* | R/Q2—Q1 | |

Of course if 25 Q×RP??, B×N wins.

White is now on the defensive and Black's superior development begins to tell. Somewhat better is 25 R/Q2—K2, and if 25 . . . , R—B8; 26 R—K8ch., R×R; 27 R×R.

| *25.* | | R—B5 |
| *26.* | P—Q5! | |

To rule out the threat of . . . , B×N.

| *26.* | | P—QR4? |

Euwe points out that Black has better moves in 26 . . . , P—N5, or 26 . . . , R/B5—B4.

| *27.* | N—Q2! | |

Now the game takes a turn in White's favor, as N—K4 is a strong threat.

| *27.* | | Q—Q5ch. |

27 . . . , R—Q5 is answered by 28 N—K4.

28. **K—R1**   **Q×QP?!**

Better is simply 28 . . . , R/B5—B2; 29 N—K4, Q×NP; 30 Q×QP—but Black sees mating possibilities by means of a combinative assault on the White King. With both players suffering from severe time pressure, Vidmar hits on a subtle refutation.

29.	**B—K4**	**R×B**
30.	**N×R**	**Q×BP**
31.	**N×QP**	**B×Pch.**
32.	**K×B**	**R—B7ch.**
33.	**K—R1**	**Q—B5**

The key to Black's combination. An apparently inescapable mate on the move is threatened, but White has seen further and now brings his own still more beautiful combination into effect.

The position has become a favorite example of ingenious recovery in a desperate situation.

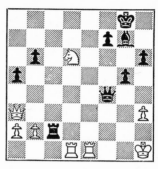

34.	**R—K8ch.**	**B—B1**

Clearly not 34 . . . , K—R2; 35 Q—Q3ch., and wins.

35.	**R×Bch.!!**	**K×R**

If 35 . . . , K—N2; 36 R×Pch. is crushing.

36.	**N—B5 dis. ch.**	**K—N1**
37.	**Q—B8ch.!!**	**Resigns**

It is mate next move. A galling resignation when he is still left threatening his own mate on the move. For this exquisite piece of play, Vidmar was awarded a brilliancy prize.

GAME 36

Alekhine—Bogolyubov

WORLD CHAMPIONSHIP MATCH, 1929

QUEEN'S GAMBIT
DECLINED

White	Black
Alekhine	Bogolyubov
1. P—Q4	N—KB3
2. P—QB4	P—B3
3. N—QB3	P—Q4
4. N—B3	P—K3
5. B—N5	QN—Q2
6. P—K4!?	

A bold method of avoiding the Cambridge Springs Defense.

6.	PXKP
7. NXP	Q—N3?!

7 . . . , B—K2 avoids the breakup of his King-side Pawns; but Bogolyubov rarely indulged in such conservative reflections.

8. NXNch.	PXN
9. B—B1	P—K4

Another dangerous move, as it portends the opening of the King file and surrenders Black's KB4 to the enemy.

10. B—Q3!?	

Sacrificing a Pawn for quick development and open lines.

10.	PXP
11. O—O	

11 Q—K2ch. can be answered by 11 . . . , N—K4 (if 12 NXN, Q—R4ch.!, and 13 . . . , QXN).

11.	B—K2

11 . . . , P—QB4 is too slow because the reply 12 R—K1ch. creates serious difficulties for Black.

12. R—K1	N—B1
13. N—R4!	B—K3
14. N—B5	B—N5

Hoping to castle on the Queen side with a good game. Black's defense requires a great fund of patience, especially in view of Alekhine's well-known resourcefulness in such situations.

In the event of 14 . . . , Q—B2, White can recover his Pawn with 15 NXB, QXN; 16 P—B4, P—KB4; 17 BXP, etc.

15. N—N7ch.!	K—Q2
16. R—K4	

From now on, this Rook displays remarkable agility.

16.	KR—N1

16 . . . , P—KB4? is answered by 17 NXP!, BXN; 18 RXPch.!

And if 16 . . . , R—Q1?; 17 P—QR3, B—K2; 18 P—QN4, K—B1; 19 P—B5, Q—B2; 20 B—KB4, and wins.

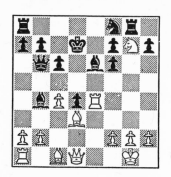

17. N—R5!?

Alekhine later recommended 17 N—B5! as best. In that case, Black's situation can easily become precarious, for example:

a) 17 . . . , B×N; 18 R× Pch., K—B1; 19 B×Bch., N—K3; 20 R—K4, etc.

b) 17 . . . , P—B4; 18 N—R6, R—N2; 19 P—QR3, B—R4; 20 P—QN4, P×P; 21 P—B5!, Q×P; 22 P×P, and 23 R×Pch., with a wide-open game that favors White's attacking prospects.

17.	B—K2
18. P—QN4!?	

Even more forcing, from the point of view of opening up lines for attack, is 18 B—B2!, P—QB4; 19 P—QN4!

18.	P—KB4!
19. P—B5!	Q×NP
20. R—K5	

The alternative 20 R—N1! is best answered by 20 . . . , Q× P; 21 R×NPch., K—K1!—but not 21 . . . , K—B1; 22 B—QR6!, P×R; 23 R—N5 dis. ch., K—Q1; 24 R×Q, B×R; 25 N—B6! followed by 26 N×KP, with a lasting attack.

20.	N—N3!

20 . . . , P—B3 is unsatisfactory, as White can reply 21 R×P!, B×R; 22 B×Bch., K—B2; 23 B—B4ch.

Another good line on 20 . . . , P—B3 is 21 R—N1, Q—R4; 22 R×Pch., K—K1 (if 22 . . . , K—B1?; 23 KR×B, N×R; 24 R×B); 23 KR×B, N×R; 24 B×P, N—B1; 25 Q—K2, etc.

21. R—N1!	Q—R4

Of course not 21 . . . , Q× R?; 22 B×Q, N×R; 23 Q×Pch. winning the Knight.

22. R—K2	P—N3

22 . . . , B×BP? is refuted by 23 N—B6ch., while 22 . . . , B×RP is answered by 23 B×Pch.

23. P×P	P×P
24. R/K2—N2	QR—N1

Black wants to keep the other Rook in reserve on the King side, but it is questionable whether his nebulous chances of counterattack outweigh the needs of defense on the other wing.

Thus, if 24 . . . , Q—Q4; 25 R×P, N—R5; 26 N—B4!, R×

128

Pch.; 27 K—B1! wins for White.

25. **B—B1**   **P—B4**

By careful play, Black has now practically consolidated his position again, and his extra Pawns begin to look formidable. White therefore plans to open up the Queen Knight and Queen Rook files to derive what advantage he can from his superior development.

26.	P—QR4!	K—B2
27.	R—N5	Q—R1
28.	P—R5!	P×P
29.	B—Q2	R×R

On 29 . . . , P—R5 White has effective replies in 30 B—R5ch. or 30 R—R5.

30.	R×R	R—N1
31.	R×P	Q—N2
32.	Q—R4	B—Q2
33.	Q—R2	Q—N6!
34.	R—R7ch.	K—Q3

Fatal is 34 . . . , K—B1?, because of 35 B—R6ch., K—Q1; 36 B—R5ch., K—K1; 37 Q×Q, R×Q; 38 R—R8ch., etc.

35.	Q—R6ch.	R—N3
36.	Q—R5	R—N2
37.	R—R6ch.	B—B3
38.	N—N7	Q—Q4

Another stage of consolidation is achieved. The King is covered and a White Bishop tied down by a mating threat.

39. **P—B3**

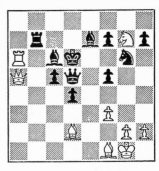

39.   K—Q2?

Black is not alive to his opportunity. By playing 39 . . . , P—Q6! he considerably reduces White's attacking chances, for example 40 Q—B3, P—B5; 41 N—K8ch., K—Q2; 42 N—B6ch., B×N; 43 Q×B, Q—B4ch.; 44 K—R1, N—K2, followed by . . . , Q—B7 or . . . , R—N8.

| 40. | B—Q3 | B—Q1 |
| 41. | Q—R1! | N—K2? |

Here he misses his last winning chance: 41 . . . , N—R5!; 42 Q—K1!, K—B1; 43 N×P!, N×N!; 44 B—K4, R—K2!

42. **N×P!**

The first Pawn is recovered elegantly. Black cannot answer with 42 . . . , N×N, for then 43 B—K4 wins.

42.		Q—N6
43.	Q—KB1	N—Q4!
44.	R—R1!	

If 44 B—QB4, Q—N8; 45 B×N, Q×Qch. (not 45 . . . ,

B×B?; 46 R—Q6ch.); 46 K×
Q, B—N4ch., winning.

| 44. | **B—QN4!** |
| 45. | **B×Bch.!** |

Not 45 R—N1?, B×B; 46
R×Q, R×R, followed by . . . ,
R—N8 or . . . , B×N and wins.

| 45. | | **Q×B** |
| 46. | **Q—K1** | |

Black has succeeded in simplifying the position and is
still a Pawn ahead; so White
now switches his attack suddenly to the other flank.

| **46.** | | **Q—B3** |
| 47. | **Q—N3!** | |

The vitality of White's attack is incredible. Bogolyubov
studied the position for sixty-
six minutes before playing:

47.		**Q—KN3**
48.	**Q—R3**	**K—B3**
49.	**N×Pch.!!**	

And with a brilliant stroke
he recovers the second Pawn.
The combination is delightfully contrived.

49.		**P×N**
50.	**Q—B8ch.**	**B—B2**
51.	**R—B1ch.**	**N—B6!**

If 51 . . . , K—N3; 52 B—

R5ch., K—R2 (not 52 . . . ,
K×B?; 53 Q×R, or 52 . . . ,
K—R3?; 53 Q—R8ch.); 53 B×
B, N×B; 54 R×N.

| 52. | **B×N** | **R—N8!** |

Not 52 . . . , P×B; 53 R×
Pch., K—N3; 54 R—N3ch., win-
ning the Rook and preventing
. . . , Q—N8ch.

| 53. | **Q—R8ch.** |

He must avoid 53 B—Q2
dis. ch., R×Rch.; 54 B×R,
Q—N8.

53.		**K—Q2**
54.	**Q—R4ch.**	**K—B1**
55.	**B—Q2**	**R×Rch.**
56.	**B×R**	**Q—Q3**

If 56 . . . , Q—N8; 57 Q—
K8ch., B—Q1; 58 Q—B6ch., or
57 . . . , K—N2; 58 Q—K4ch.
The game is now an inevitable
draw. No world championship
match ever produced a finer
struggle than this.

57.	**Q—K8ch.**	**K—N2**
58.	**Q—N5ch.**	**K—R2**
59.	**Q—R4ch.**	**K—N2**
60.	**Q—N5ch.**	**B—N3**
61.	**Q—Q3**	**Q—N3**
62.	**Q×Q**	**BP×Q**
63.	**K—B2**	**K—B3**
	Drawn	

Stoltz—Colle

BLED, 1931

Gosta Stoltz (born 1910) is a Swedish master who made his debut in international play about 1930 and has substantial tournament and match successes to his credit.

Edgard Colle (1897–1932) was a brilliant Belgian master whose name is particularly associated with the form of the Queen's Pawn Game named after him. He won the international tournaments at Meran, 1926, and Scarborough, 1930.

ALEKHINE'S DEFENSE

	White	Black
	Stoltz	Colle
1.	P–K4	N–KB3
2.	P–K5	N–Q4
3.	P–QB4	N–N3
4.	P–B5	N–Q4
5.	N–QB3	NxN
6.	QPxN	N–B3?

The normal line against the Lasker treatment of this defense is 6 . . . , P–Q3. Black's optimistic attempt to use the advanced White Pawn as a target recoils horribly on him.

| 7. | N–B3 | P–KN3? |
| 8. | B–QB4 | B–N2 |

By his previous move, Black has virtually committed himself to . . . , P–Q3 rather than . . . , P–K3, yet after White's reply he will be unable to play . . . , P–Q3 without losing a Pawn.

| 9. | B–B4 | O–O |
| 10. | Q–Q2 | P–N3 |

Now the only possible development for the Queen Bishop, but Black is not allowed time to play . . . , B–N2.

| 11. | P–KR4! | P–KR4 |

Black is already in trouble, for he is faced with a series of moves such as P–R5 followed by an exchange of Pawns and B–KR6, with mating intentions by White.

| 12. | O–O–O | |

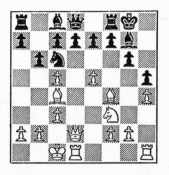

12.   **P—K3**

A sad necessity, as his last move has only created a new attacking target for White. The immediate threat was 13 Q—B2 (menace: 14 Q×P), K—R1; 14 P—K6.

After 12 . . . , P×P, White gets a vicious attack with 13 P—KN4!, for example: 13 . . . , P×P; 14 P—R5!, P×N; 15 P× P, P—K3; 16 B—KN5, Q—K1; 17 B—B6, N×P; 18 R—R8ch.!!, B×R; 19 Q—R6, N×P; 20 R— R1! forcing mate.

13. **B—KN5!**   **P—B3**

Now his King Knight Pawn will be gravely weakened, but if 13 . . . , Q—K1; 14 B—B6!, and Black can hardly play 14 . . . , B×B; 15 P×B, K—R2 (directed again 16 Q—R6); 16 B—Q3, threatening 17 Q—N5 and 18 Q×RPch.

14. **KP×P**   **B×P**
15. **Q—B2**   **Q—K1**

The only defense against the two threats of Q×Pch. and B×Pch.

16. **B—Q3**   **K—N2**

Now White will open up new attacking lines.

17. **P—KN4!**   **RP×P**
18. **QR—N1!**

White prosecutes the attack vigorously. If now 18 . . . , P×N; 19 B×P! with decisive effect.

18.   **B×Bch.!**
19. **N×B**   **N—K4!**
20. **B—K4**   **B—R3!**

In his almost hopeless position, Black must go all out or go under, so having temporarily stopped the King-side attack, he offers a sacrifice of the exchange.

21. **B×R?**

White's attack has brought him a gain of material, but he would be better advised not to take it, for it means abandoning all pressure to Black.

It was not easy to see in the heat of the battle that White can strengthen his attack decisively with the subtle move 21 P—QB4!!, for example:

a) 21 . . . , N×P; 22 R×P followed by P—R5.

b) 21 . . . , B×P; 22 Q— B3!, P—Q3; 23 R×P and White has a luxurious choice of threats: 24 P—B4 or 24 P— R5 or 24 B×R, followed by 25 R—K1.

21.   N—Q6ch.!
22. K—N1   Q×B!

Not 22 . . . , R×P?; 23 Q—
R4!, R×Pch. (or 23 . . . , N×
BP; 24 Q—Q4ch.); 24 K—R1,
B—N4; 25 Q×RP, B—B5; 26
R—N2!, winning.

23. P—QB4

Black was threatening to
regain the exchange by 23
. . . , N×BP.

23.   N—K4
24. Q—B3   R—B4
25. P—B4?

He wants to play R—K1,
which at the moment is no
threat because of the reply 25
. . . , K—N1, when 26 R×N
is answered by 26 . . . , Q×
Rch. Stoltz therefore evolves a
problemlike maneuver to induce Black to block the diagonal himself. But unfortunately
it is not quite sound, and
Black is given a strong passed
Pawn.

Better is the slower line 25
P—N3, etc.

25.   P×P e.p.
26. R—K1

This seems decisive, for if
26 . . . , K—B3; 27 R×N, R×
R; 28 R—K1, P—Q3; 29 N×
BP, and wins.

Or 26 . . . , P—Q3; 27 N×
Pch., K—B2; 28 N×P, Q—N2;
29 N×B, Q×N; 30 P×QP,
likewise winning.

26.   P—B7!!
27. R×N

The first point of the combination as White saw it. If
now 27 . . . , Q×Rch.; 28 R—
K1 dis. ch. wins.

27.   K—N1!!

After this quiet move, Black
must win at least a Rook!

28. R—KB1!   Q—N7!
29. Q—Q3

The second point of the
combination as White saw it.
The threat against both Rooks
is met, for if now 29 . . . ,
R×R; 30 Q×Pch. and mates.

White's move is inadequate,
however, and the same is true
of 29 Q—B1, R×R, threatening 30 . . . , Q×R followed
by . . . , R—K8ch.—or 29 Q—
KR3, R×N; 30 Q×Q, R×Q;
31 R—K2, B×P, and the ending is won for Black.

29.   B×P!!

The real point of Black's
combination, and a beautiful
one.

30. Q×B   R×R
31. Q—Q3   Q×Rch.!
     Resigns

An object lesson in refusing
to reconcile oneself to im-
pending resignation, however
hopeless the situation may
appear. A game is never lost
until it is won.

GAME 38

Colle—Kashdan

BLED, 1931

Isaac Kashdan (born 1905), on of the leading American masters, scored an exceptional series of successes in the early 1930's.

QUEEN'S PAWN
OPENING

White	Black
Colle	Kashdan
1. P–Q4	P–Q4
2. N–KB3	N–KB3
3. P–K3	P–B4
4. P–B3	P–K3

Colle is playing his famous system, with which he won many brilliant games.

5. QN–Q2	N–B3
6. B–Q3	B–Q3
7. O–O	O–O
8. PXP	BXP
9. P–K4	

The key move of Colle's method of attack.

9.	Q–B2
10. PXP	

Though this gives Black an isolated Pawn, it is not consistent with the scheme of attack, which requires the use of the square K4. Better is 10 Q–K2, in the hope of inducing Black to play . . . , PXP to avoid P–K5.

10.	PXP!

Black does not mind getting an isolated Pawn, as his pieces come into action very favorably.

11. N–N3	B–N3
12. Q–B2	R–K1

12 . . . , B–N5 is a promising alternative.

13. B–KN5	N–K5
14. QR–K1	B–KB4
15. B–K3	B–N3
16. N–R4!?	

Intending N×B followed by B×B, whereupon he can win a Pawn. Better, from the viewpoint of practical play, is the positional course 16 B×B, Q× B; 17 QN–Q4.

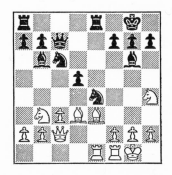

16.   N×KBP!!?

It seems unbelievable that this capture is possible, in view of the fact that the captured Pawn was protected no less than four times! The sacrifice does not lead to anything like a forced win, but White's defense is inordinately difficult and he has many ways to go wrong.

17. B×N

On 17 Q×N, QB×B, Black is a Pawn ahead; and on 17 R×N?, KB×B wins the exchange. Kashdan analyzes the other possibilities as follows:

a) 17 K×N, Q—B5ch.; 18 N—B3, R×B; 19 R×R, Q×Rch.; 20 K—N3, B×B, and wins.

b) 17 QB×B, Q×B; 18 R×Rch., R×R; 19 B×B (if 19 R×N?, R—K8ch.!), N—K5 dis. ch.; 20 K—R1, RP×B with, material and positional advantage.

c) 17 KB×B, N—KN5!; 18 B×BPch., K—R1; 19 P—N3, N×B winning at least the exchange.

17.   B×Bch.
18. K×B

Again forced!

18.   Q—N3ch.
19. K—N3

Still having no choice; for 19 N—Q4?, N×N; 20 P×N, Q×Pch. is quite hopeless for White; while after 19 K—B3,

N—K4ch.; 20 R×N, R×R, Black's attack is still going full force, a two-move mate being threatened.

19.   R—K6ch.
20. R×R   Q×Rch.
21. R—B3   Q—N4ch.

Kashdan had anticipated playing 21 . . . , B×B; 22 R×Q, B×Q, with an easy win; but on 21 . . . , B×B? White simply replies 22 Q×B!

The text keeps up the pressure, and while White is far from lost, his life is miserable enough.

22. K—R3   N—K4
23. R—N3

The attempt to beat off the attack by surrendering the exchange with 23 P—N3? fails after 23 . . . , Q—N5ch.; 24 K—N2, N×B; 25 R×N, Q—K5ch., and wins.

23.   Q—R3!

24. B—B5!?

By no means the losing move, as has been claimed.

The simplest course is 24 B×B, N×B (not 24 . . . , RP× B?; 25 Q—Q2! and wins); 25 R—N4, N—K4; 26 Q—B5! or 26 Q—K2! (but not 26 R—N3?, P—KN4!) with a very promising game for White.

24.   **R—K1!**

The immediate . . ̇. , B—R4 (intending . . . , P—KN4) will not do because of 25 Q—Q2! seizing the initiative.

25.   **N—Q4**

Not 25 Q—Q2??, B×Bch. and wins.

Also unsatisfactory is 25 B× B, N×B!; 26 R—N4 because of 26 . . . , R—K6ch.; 27 P— N3, N×N!; 28 R×N, Q— K3ch.!; 29 R—N4 (forced), P—KR4, with an easy win.

25.   **B—R4!**
26.   **Q—B2?**

There is a swindling possibility in 26 Q—R4 (26 . . . , P—B3?; 27 B—N6!), but after 26 . . . , R—KB1 White remains under severe pressure.

Another inadequate line is 26 B—N4 (or 26 N/Q4—B3, B×N; 27 P×N, P—KN4), B× Bch.; 27 R×B, N×R; 28 K×N, R—K5ch., and wins.

Best, however, is 26 B×Pch.!, restoring material equality after 26 . . . , Q×B; 27 Q× Qch., K×Q; 28 N/R4—B5, and leaving White with the better game.

Likewise after 26 B×Pch.!, K—B1; 27 Q—B5, B—N5ch.

(there seems to be nothing better); 28 R×B, N×R; 29 Q×N (not 29 K×N?, R— K5ch.), Q×B, White has the better of it.

26.   **P—KN4!**

Now Black wins his piece back.

27.   **B×Pch.**

On 27 Q—K3!? Black simply replies 27 . . . , P—B3! followed by the removal of his King.

But it would be a serious mistake to play 27 . . . , P— N5ch.? (in reply to 27 Q— K3!?); 28 B×P, Q×Q (worse yet is 28 . . . , B×Bch.??; 29 R×Bch., winning right off); 29 B×B dis. ch., Q×Rch.; 30 K×Q, and White should win.

27.   **K—B1!**

Not 27 . . . , Q×B; 28 R× Pch.—or 27 . . . , K×B; 28 Q—B5ch., B—N3; 29 Q×NP, etc.

28.   **B—B5**   **P×N**
29.   **R—K3**   **R—K2!**

A beautiful move, to prevent White from capturing the Rook with a check, and so threatening . . . , N—N3 (or . . . , N—N5).

30.   **R—K1**

If instead 30 Q—K1, N—N3!; 31 R×R, N—B5ch.; 32 K×P, N×Pch.; 33 K—N3 (if 33 K— R3, B—B6 dis. ch.; 34 K—N3,

Q—B5ch., etc.), Q—N4ch.; 34
K—B2, N×Q; 35 R×N, Q—
R5ch.; 36 K—B1, Q×P, with
an easy win.

If 30 N—K2, N—N5! wins.

If 30 N—B2, Q—N4; 31 P—
KN3, B—N5ch.; 32 B×B, N×B,
winning.

| 30. | | B—N5ch.! |

Another fine move that
forces the exchange of
Queens, without which the
game would still be difficult
to win.

| 31. | B×B | N—Q6! |
| 32. | Q×P | N—B5ch.! |

A delightful finesse to pick
up a Pawn.

33.	K—N3	Q×Qch.
34.	K×Q	N×Pch.
35.	K—N5	R×R

The end of a gripping tactical struggle.

36.	P—KR4	N—K6
37.	B—B3	N—B5
38.	N—B5	R—N8ch.
39.	K—B4	R—KB8
40.	N—K3	R—B7
41.	N—Q1	R—R7
42.	P—R5	N×P
43.	N—K3	N—Q6ch.
44.	K—N3	R×QRP
45.	N×P	R—N7
46.	P—R6	N—K4
47.	K—B4	N—N3ch.
48.	K—K4	P—N3
49.	N—B6	N—K2
	Resigns	

Euwe—Yates

HASTINGS, 1931–32

Fred D. Yates (1884–1932) was many times British champion and a frequent competitor in international tournaments. His style displayed great tenacity and determination, and in his finest games he rose to extraordinary heights of sustained brilliancy. Though he was not sufficiently consistent to win the highest prizes, he won notable victories from almost every great master of his time.

KING'S INDIAN
DEFENSE

White	Black
Euwe	Yates
1. P–Q4	N–KB3
2. P–QB4	P–KN3
3. N–QB3	B–N2
4. P–K4	P–Q3
5. P–B3	

One of the most aggressive lines against this defense. The idea is to castle Queen side, in conjunction with P–KN4 and P–KR4.

5.	O–O
6. B–K3	N–B3
7. KN–K2	P–K4
8. Q–Q2	

Here or next move, P–Q5 is the most straightforward course.

8.	N–Q2
9. O–O–O	

More in keeping with the usual forms of the opening is 9 P–Q5, N–K2; 10 P–KN4, followed by 11 N–N3.

9.	N–N3
10. P–QN3	

Rather than block his King Knight Pawn with N–N3, White prefers to create a weakness in his castled position, which he does not estimate as too serious.

10.	P–QR4?!

Beginning a sacrificial combination that is more enterprising than sound.

11. PxP	

This looks like the refutation of Black's plans, for if 11 . . . , PxP; 12 QxQ, RxQ; 13 RxRch., NxR; 14 BxN, PxB; 15 N–Q5 and Black's Queen side has been fatally weakened.

11.	P–R5!?

Since some loss of material is inevitable, Yates grimly goes ahead with his plan.

12. BxN	RPxP!?
13. B–K3	

Stronger was 13 RP×P when Black could hardly risk 13 . . . , P×B but would have to try 13 . . . , B×P; 14 B—K3, N—R4; 15 Q—B2, with variations similar to those in the actual game. There would be this difference, however: the presence of the extra Pawn on QN3 would give White's position a solidity that it does not have in the actual continuation.

13.		NP×P
14.	N×P	B×P
15.	N/K2—B3	B—K3
16.	P—B4	N—R4!

Gaining time for the attack. At considerable cost Black has managed to work up a persistent pressure that is difficult to contend with in over-the-board play.

17.	Q—QB2	B—N2
18.	N—Q5	P—QB3!

White's Knight is too strongly posted at Q5. Yates plans a further sacrifice to dislodge the advanced Knight.

19.	B—N6!	Q—N1!
20.	N—B7	P—Q4!
21.	P—K5	

The closing of the long diagonal is of questionable value, as will be seen. More effective is 21 N×B, P×N; 22 P—N3.

21.		B—B4

Obvious enough, but nevertheless a puzzling move to answer properly.

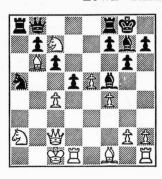

22. B—Q3!

Best; on 22 Q—R4, remarkable variations result from 22 . . . , N×P!:

a) 23 Q×R, N×B!; 24 Q×Q, R×Q. Black wins the Knight, remaining with two strong passed Pawns.

b) 23 N×R, Q×P!!; 24 P×Q, B—R3ch.; 25 R—Q2, B×Rch.; 26 K—Q1, N—N7ch.; 27 K×B, N×Q, and Black must win one of the hanging pieces, when he has winning chances with three passed Pawns for a piece.

22.		B×B
23.	R×B	N×P
24.	N×R	Q×N
25.	B—Q4	R—B1!

Hoping for a rapid advance of his three passed Pawns, the only way 'he can secure compensation for the Rook down.

26. R—K1

On 26 P—K6, B×B; 27 P×Pch., K×P; 28 R×B, Q—R6ch.; 29 K—N1, Q—B4, and the double threat of . . . , N—R6ch.

or . . . , Q×R forces White to give up the exchange. 30 Q–Q3? or 30 Q–Q1?? will not do because of 30 . . . , Q–N3ch. or . . . , Q–N4ch.

26.		P–QB4
27.	B–R1	P–QN4
28.	R–K2	P–N5
29.	Q–N3	

Allowing Yates to bring off a very pretty combination that banishes all possibility of losing.

29.		N×P!!

If this Knight is captured, 30 . . . , P–B5 wins White's Queen or *both* his Rooks!

30.	R×P	P–B5
31.	Q–KR3	

Forced; but now Black sets up a triple fork!

31.		N–Q6ch.
32.	K–N1	N×P

The culmination of his Knight maneuvers. At first sight he seems to recover a whole Rook with a won end-

ing, but White discovers an ingenious move to remain a minor piece ahead.

33.	R–QR5!	N×Q

Likewise after 33 . . . , Q–B3!; 34 Q–K3 (not 34 N×P?, R–N1), N×R; 35 B×B, K×B; 36 Q×N, White can hold the position.

34.	R×Q	R×R
35.	B×B	K×B
36.	P×N	P–N6
37.	N–B3	

After a dazzling display of Knight maneuvering by Black, we get an equally effective performance by the White Knight.

37.		R–Q1
38.	K–N2	R–Q6
39.	N–R4	R×P
40.	N–N6	P–N4
41.	N×P	P–B4
42.	N–Q2	K–B3
43.	N×P	

A draw is now the legitimate outcome.

43.		P–R4
44.	K–B2	P–B5
45.	N–Q4	P–R5
46.	K–Q2	R–R6
47.	K–K1	P–R6
48.	R–K6ch.	K–B2
49.	R–K5	K–N3
50.	N–K2	R–R7
51.	K–B2	K–B3
52.	R–B5	P–N5
53.	R–B4	P–B6
54.	R×P	P×N
55.	R–KR4	Drawn

GAME 40

Spielmann—Lasker

MOSCOW, 1935

Rudolf Spielmann (1884–1942) was one of the masters who began to make a name for themselves early in the twentieth century. In style he was a romantic and reverted to the gambits of an earlier age. His greatest success was winning the important tournament at Semmering, 1926. He was an Austrian.

SCOTCH GAME

	White	Black
	Spielmann	Lasker
1.	P–K4	P–K4
2.	N–KB3	N–QB3
3.	P–Q4	PXP
4.	NXP	N–B3
5.	N–QB3	B–N5
6.	NXN	NPXN
7.	B–Q3	P–Q4
8.	PXP	Q–K2ch.

This is usually played for drawing purposes, but Lasker, as so often in his games, seeks to bring about a difficult game in the hope of outmaneuvering his opponent.

| 9. | Q–K2 | QXQch.!? |

9 . . . , NXP is the drawish move.

10.	KXQ	PXP
11.	N–N5!	K–Q1
12.	R–Q1	P–B3
13.	P–QB3	R–K1ch.

Despite the previous exchanges, Black's defense is by no means a simple matter. If 13 . . . , PXN; 14 PXB, P–

QR3; 15 B–N5, threatening 16 B–B2 and 17 B–N3.

14.	K–B1	B–B1
15.	N–Q4	K–B2
16.	B–B4ch.	K–N3?!

In playing this move, Lasker is literally looking for trouble, as 16 . . . , B–Q3; 17 BXBch., KXB; 18 N–B5ch., BXN; 19 BXB leads to the draw that he is trying to avoid.

| 17. | P–QR4 | P–QR4 |
| 18. | P–QN4! | |

With the better game, White feels justified in playing to open up the position. The resulting attack is very powerful despite the absence of the Queens.

| 18. | | PXP |

Black does not have much choice. Thus if 18 . . . , B–Q2?; 19 PXPch., RXP (not 19 . . . , K–B4??; 20 N–N3 mate, or 19 . . . , KXP??; 20 B–B7 mate!); 20 KR–N1ch., K–R2; 21 B–B7, trapping the Queen Rook.

19. **P–R5ch.!   K–N2**

And not 19 . . . , R×P??; 20 R×R, K×R; 21 B–B7ch., K–R5; 22 R–R1 mate.

20. **P×P   N–K5**

This allows a pretty sacrificial continuation, but Lasker is an old hand at such situations. He knows that in a complicated situation he has some chance, and in a passive situation none at all. Thus, after 20 . . . , B×P; 21 KR–N1, P–B4; 22 N–B2, or 20 . . . , B–Q2; 21 QR–N1, followed by 22 P–N5, White has powerful pressure without incurring the slightest risk.

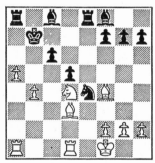

21. **N×P!!**

Very pretty. If now 21 . . . , K×N; 22 QR–B1ch., K–Q2 (or 22 . . . , K–N2; 23 R–B7ch., K–N1; 24 R–K7 dis. ch., and mate follows); 23 B–N5ch., K–K2 (if 23 . . . , K–Q1; 24 R×Pch., etc.); 24 R–B7ch., K–Q1; 25 R×Pch., and wins.

21.   **P–N4!?**

Trying to create a diversion. He wants to force White's Bishop off its diagonal, whereupon the situation of the sacrificial Knight will become precarious.

22. **B×N   R×B**

Keeping up the threats. If 22 . . . , QP×B; 23 N–Q8ch., R×N; 24 R×R, B–K2; 25 R–K8, B–B3; 26 B–K5, with an easy win.

23. **N–Q8ch.   K–R3**
24. **B×P?**

Missing a brilliant win by 24 R×P!!, R×B; 25 P–N5ch., K–R2; 26 R–B1!, and Black cannot hold the game:

  a) 26 . . . , R–B3; 27 R–B7ch., K–N1; 28 P–N6.

  b) 26 . . . , B–QN2; 27 N×B, K×N; 28 R–Q7ch., K–N1; 29 P–R6!, etc.

  c) 26 . . . , K–N1; 27 P–N6, B–QN5; 28 R×Bch.!, K×R; 29 P–N7ch., etc.

24.   **B–K3**

He cannot take the Knight Pawn yet, for then 25 N×P leaves White two Pawns ahead.

25. **N–B6!**

After 25 N×B, P×N; 26 B–Q2, B×P; 27 B×B, R×B, White's winning possibilities are reduced to a minimum.

Black is two Pawns down, without any visible form of compensation. Lasker's determined defense borders on the miraculous.

142   SPIELMANN—LASKER

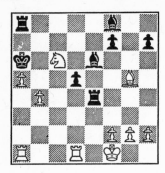

25.   B—N2!

Black's Bishops are now
effectively in play.
25 . . . , B×P? is very poor
because of 26 QR—N1!:
    a) 26 . . . , B×P?; 27 N×
B, K×N; 28 R—R1ch., R—R5;
29 R×Rch., K×R; 30 R—R1ch.,
winning a Rook.
    b) 26 . . . , B—QB4 (if 26
. . . , B—KB1??; 27 R—N6
mate); 27 B—K7!, B—R2; 28
N—N4ch., with a winning
position.
    c) 26 . . . , K—N4; 27 N—
Q4ch., K—B5 (if 27 . . . , K—
B4; 28 B—K7ch. wins or 27
. . . , K—R5; 28 R—R1ch., B—
R6; 29 B—B1 winning); 28
QR—B1ch., B—B6; 29 N—K2,
P—Q5; 30 P—B3, R—K4; 31
R×Pch., winning the Bishop.

26. QR—B1   R—QB5
27. B—K3?

The best course seems 27
R×R!, P×R; 28 N—Q4, B×N;
29 R×B, K—N4; 30 B—Q2,
and White's connected passed
plus-Pawns should decide the

issue in his favor despite the
Bishops on opposite colors.
27.   K—N4
28. N—R7ch.

Even here 28 N—Q4ch., B×
N; 29 B×B, R×R; 30 R×R,
K×P; 31 B—N6, offers some
winning chances—consider-
ably decreased, of course,
when White is reduced to one
extra Pawn.

28.   K×P
29. B—N6

Black has successfully sur-
vived the first phase. The
struggle will now center
around the Queen Rook Pawn.

29.   R—B6!
30. R—N1ch.   R—N6
31. N—B6ch.   K—R5

The calmness with which
Lasker maneuvers in the midst
of manifold dangers is inspir-
ing. Spielmann finally realizes
that he cannot accomplish
anything with his passed Pawn
unless he breaks the diagonal
of Black's King Bishop.

32. B—Q4   R×R
33. R×R   B×B
34. N×B   R—R3

The Rook Pawn is still
taboo, for if 34 . . . , R×P?;
35 R—R1ch., K—N5; 36 N—
B6ch. wins the Rook.

35. R—R1ch.   K—N5
36. K—K2

36 N×B, P×N; 37 P—N4!
may be better. In that case,

Black still cannot win the Queen Rook Pawn, as White makes a Queen on the King side. And even 37 . . . , K–B6; 38 P–R4, K–N7; 39 R–K1! leaves Black with a hard fight ahead of him.

36.   **B–Q2**

Now White should continue 37 K–Q3, B–R5 (37 . . . , R×P?; 38 N–B2ch., K–N4; 39 R×Rch., K×R; 40 K–Q4 wins for White); 38 R–QB1, R×P; 39 N–B6ch., B×N; 40 R×B, R–R7; 41 R–B6, and Black still has to struggle for the draw.

37. **N–B2ch.?**

After this feeble move, it is White who is in danger of losing!

37.	**K–B6**
38. **N–K3**	**B–N4ch.**
39. **K–K1**	**P–Q5**
40. **R–B1ch.**	

Now if 40 N–Q5ch.??, K–N7; 41 R–Q1, R–K3ch.; 42 K–Q2, R–K7 mate!

40.   **K–Q6**

Not 40 . . . , K–N7?; 41 R–B5! when Black must not play 41 . . . , R×P??; 42 N–B4ch., and wins–or 41 . . . , P×N?; 42 R×Bch., and White wins the ending.

41. **R–Q1ch.**

After 41 R–B5, B–R5; 42 N–B5, R–K3ch., there are still chances for White to go wrong.

41.   **K–B6**
                       Drawn

White has adequate counterplay after 41 . . . , K–K5; 42 N–B2, P–Q6; 43 P–B3ch.! K–K4; 44 N–N4, R–Q3; 45 P–R6, etc., or 43 . . . , K–B5; 44 N–Q4, B–B5; 45 R–B1, etc.

Black's last move (41 . . . , K–B6) would result in a draw by repetition of moves–a worthy conclusion to a game that was in the balance up to the very last move.

GAME 41

Horowitz—Trifunovich

INTERNATIONAL TEAM TOURNAMENT, WARSAW, 1935

Israel A. Horowitz (born 1907), is one of the leading American masters and has published Chess Review *since 1933.*

Dr. Petar Trifunovich (born 1910) has enjoyed the distinction of being one of the leading Yugoslav masters for many years. He has won numerous prizes in master tournaments, and has to his credit a drawn match with Najdorf.

DUTCH DEFENSE

White	Black
Horowitz	Trifunovich
1. P–Q4	P–K3
2. P–QB4	P–KB4
3. P–KN3	N–KB3
4. B–N2	B–N5ch.
5. N–Q2	P–Q4

The Stonewall formation is rather illogical in connection with . . . , B–N5ch., which foreshadows the disappearance of the black-squared Bishop.

6. N–B3	N–B3

Another "nonthematic" move, but Black is playing to win a Pawn. White is quite willing to take the dare, and an intricate struggle is the consequence.

7. O–O	O–O
8. P–QR3!?	B×N
9. Q×B	P×P

This ought to be bad "on principle." But what gives it at least an air of plausibility,

is that White's Queen Pawn requires guarding. This hampers White in his efforts to regain the Pawn.

Thus, if he plays 10 Q–B3, P–QN4; 11 P–QR4, N–K5, his position becomes very awkward. Also after 10 Q–B3, P–QN4; 11 N–K5 (apparently very strong), N×P! is an embarrassing reply.

10. R–Q1	N–K5
11. Q–B2	P–QN4

Black seems to have carried out his aim perfectly, and White is hard put to it to regain his Pawn or devise compensating complications. For example: 12 P–QR4, N–N5; 13 Q–N1, P–B3; 14 P×P, P×P; 15 N–Q2, N×N!; 16 B×N, N–Q4, and White has nothing to show for his Pawn minus.

However, White has an astonishing reply that establishes a clear positional advantage for him. Black's extra Pawn proves worthless under the circumstances.

144

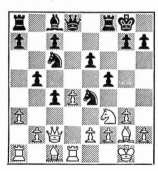

12. N–N5!!   N×N

The alternative procedure was 12 . . . , N×QP; 13 B×N! with these possibilities:

a) 13 . . . , N×Q; 14 R× Q, R×R; 15 B×N!, with two minor pieces for Rook and two Pawns. With the Bishop pair and with the breakup possibilities inherent in P–QR4, White has the better of it.

b) 13 . . . , P×B; 14 Q× KP, N–B6ch.; 15 P×N!, Q× Rch.; 16 K–N2, P–N3 (or 16 . . . , Q–Q6; 17 Q×R, P–KR3; 18 N–R3, P–K4; 19 Q–K4); 17 Q×R, P–KR3; 18 N–R3, P–K4; 19 P–KN4, P–N4 (not 19 . . . , B×P?; 10 Q×Rch.!); 20 Q–K4 and wins.

13. KB×N   R–N1

White has a clear initiative now that should soon make it possible for him to regain the Pawn. All this he owes to the power of the fianchettoed Bishop on the long diagonal.

14. P–QR4!   P–B5
15. B–N2   BP×P

16. KRP×P   P–QR3
17. P×P   P×P
18. R–R7

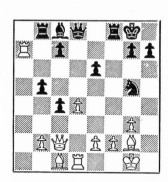

Black feels uncomfortably menaced, and he cannot manage to shake off the pressure without returning his booty. If 18 . . . , N–B2; 19 B–B4, N–Q3; 20 P–Q5! with these possibilities:

a) 20 . . . , P×P; 21 B× Pch., K–R1; 22 B–K4, P–R3; 23 Q–Q2! (even stronger than 23 R×P!?, R×B!; 24 R×B, R×R; 25 P×R, Q–B3, etc.).

b) 20 . . . , K–R1; 21 P–N3!, R–B2; 22 B×N, Q×B; 23 QP×P, Q×P; 24 B–Q5, and wins.

In these and similar variations, White's superior development always makes itself felt.

18.   P–B3
19. B×N

Not 19 B×P?, N–R6ch.

19.   Q×B
20. B×P   Q–B3!

Now that White has added material equality to positional superiority, Black must find counterplay.

| 21. | P—K3 | P—K4 |
| 22. | B—Q5ch. | K—R1 |

Avoiding a disastrous pin: if 22 . . . , B—K3?; 23 P×P, Q×P; 24 Q—B3!! wins a piece.

23.	PXP	QXP
24.	Q—B3!	QXQ
25.	PXQ	B—B4!

Prevents R—N1 and practically forces White's reply, which exposes him to serious danger.

| 26. | P—K4 | B—N5 |
| 27. | R—N1! | B—B6 |

Now the threat is . . . , R—N3—R3. White has a won ending if he can parry this threat.

| 28. | R—N7! | RXR |
| 29. | BXR | |

White need not fear 29 . . . , R—B3 because of 30 P—K5!

| 29. | | R—Q1 |

His Queen Knight Pawn is momentarily untouchable.

| 30. | B—Q5! | P—N4 |

Or 30 . . . , R—QN1; 31 B×P, B×P; 32 R×P, R—QB1; 33 R—N4, and White wins the ending in due course.

31.	RXP	R—K1
32.	P—K5!	BXB
33.	RXB	P—N5

To stop P—B4. But now Black will soon have to lose a second Pawn.

34.	R—B5	P—R4
35.	P—K6	K—N2
36.	RXRP	K—B3
37.	R—B5	RXP
38.	RXP	R—K8ch.
39.	K—N2	K—B4
40.	R—B8	R—QB8
41.	P—QB4	K—K3
42.	P—B5	R—B5
43.	P—B6	K—Q3
44.	R—B8!	KXP
45.	R—B8ch.	K—Q4
46.	RXR	KXR
47.	P—B3	K—Q4
48.	PXP	K—K4
49.	K—R3	K—B3
50.	K—R4	Resigns

An extraordinarily difficult game, which takes on added value from the notable tenacity of Black's resistance.

Pleci–Fenoglio

MAR DEL PLATA, 1936

Isaias Pleci and Virgilio Fenoglio are two outstanding Argentine masters.

SICILIAN DEFENSE
(in effect)

	White	Black
	Pleci	Fenoglio
1.	P–QB4	P–QB4
2.	N–QB3	N–QB3
3.	N–B3	N–B3
4.	P–Q4	PXP
5.	NXP	P–KN3
6.	P–K4	B–N2

Black has transposed into a variation of the Sicilian Defense that is highly unfavorable for him. White centralizes very powerfully on Q4 and Q5, not only cramping Black's game badly but leaving him with discouragingly meager possibilities for the deployment of his Rooks.

7.	B–K3	P–Q3
8.	B–K2	B–K3
9.	O–O	O–O
10.	K–R1	Q–B1
11.	R–B1	

There is some careful reflection behind this obvious-looking move. For instance: 11 . . . , NXN; 12 BXN, BXP; 13 BXB! (if 13 N–Q5, Black extricates himself with . . . ,

BXB!), QXB; 14 N–Q5, QXP; 15 R–R1, Q–B5; 16 P–QN3, Q–N4; 17 N–B7, Q–Q2; 18 NXR, RXN; 19 P–B3, P–QR3; 20 R–B1, and occupation of the Queen Bishop file will decide in White's favor, despite the approximate material equivalence of two Pawns for the exchange.

11.		N–KN5

Forcing an exchange and thus hoping to free his game somewhat.

| 12. | BXN | |

Best (if 12 NXB?, NXB with advantage to Black).

12.		BXB
13.	P–B3	B–Q2

Or 13 . . . , B–K3; 14 N–Q5!, QBXN?; 15 BPXB, and wins.

| 14. | N–Q5! | |

This powerful centralizing move, so characteristic of the variation, not only menaces Black with instant catastrophe (threat: 15 NXN), but creates a difficult situation for him in

general: the Knight can only
be driven off by weakening
the Queen Pawn irreparably
with . . . , P—K3.

14.	Q—Q1
15. Q—Q2	R—B1

Black's desire to get this
Rook in play is quite natural,
but the move creates more
problems than it solves.

16. N—N5!

A very awkward thrust for
Black to parry. If 16 . . . , P—
QR3; 17 B—N6, Q—K1; 18
N/N5—B7 wins; or if 16 . . . ,
P—N3; 17 N×RP!, N×N; 18
B×P, etc.

16.   N—K4

The alternative . . . , R—R1
leaves Black with an unbear-
ably passive game.

17. P—QN3	B×N
18. P×B	R×R

Unavoidable, for if 18 . . . ,
P—N3?; 19 R×R wins at once.
Or if 18 . . . , P—K3? still 19
R×R, etc.

If 18 . . . , R—R1; 19 R—B7,
P—K3; 20 N—K7ch., K—R1;
21 R×P wins. But after 18
. . . , R—R1, it would be wrong
to play 19 N—B7, R—B1; 20
B×P, R×N; 21 B—N6, R×R!

19. R×R

Black is now in a desperate
situation, as White's formidable combination of the
Knight on Q5 and the Rook

on the open Queen Bishop file
threatens to culminate decisively in R—B7.

19.   P—K3

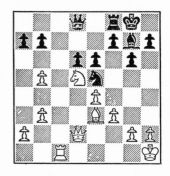

20. B—N5!   Q—N1

At first sight a curious reply.
The obvious retort is 20 . . . ,
P—B3, seemingly winning a
piece. But there follows 21
R—B8!, Q—Q2 forced; 22 N×
Pch., B×N; 23 R×Rch., K×R;
24 B×B with a winning position (24 . . . , Q×P?; 25 Q×
Pch., and Black must not play
25 . . . , K—B2 because of
mate in two).

21. N—B6ch.

Thus White has retained his
advantage. He has to part
with his powerful Knight, but
he obtains the gratifying compensation of devastating mastery of the black squares, plus
the win of the feeble Queen
Pawn.

21.   B×N

Forced (if 21 . . . , K—R1?;
22 P—B4).

22. B×B

The threat of mate by Q–R6 now wins the Queen Pawn.

22.   R–B1

Or 22 . . . , N–Q2; 23 B–K7, etc.

23. R–Q1   N–Q2

White was still threatening Q–R6.

24. B–K7   Q–B2
25. B×P   Q–B7

Threatening 26 . . . , Q×Q; 27 R×Q, R–B8ch., and mate follows.

26. P–KR4   Q×Q
27. R×Q   N–N3

The ending is not easy for White, as his extra Pawn is doubled. The play that follows is exceedingly instructive. White's first requirement is to bring about an exchange of Rooks, to prevent any marauding expeditions against his Queen-side Pawns, and to be able to assert the superiority of his Bishop over the Knight.

28. B–K5   K–B1
29. B–B6   K–K1
30. K–R2!

The King is headed for a fatal irruption among the Black King-side Pawns.

30.   N–Q2
31. B–Q4   P–N3
32. K–N3   K–K2
33. B–N2   K–K1

34. B–R3   R–B2
35. K–B4   N–B4

After 35 . . . , P–KR3; 36 B–Q6, R–B1; 37 P–K5, White plays K–K4 and P–KN4, followed by P–B4 and an eventual break-through with P–R5.

36. R–Q6   N–N2
37. R–B6!

Now White has a crystal-clear winning method, as the exchange of Rooks is forced (37 . . . , R–Q2; 38 R–B8ch., N–Q1; 39 K–K3, R–Q8; 40 B–N2, with an easy win).

37.   R×R
38. P×R   N–R4
39. P–B7   K–Q2
40. K–K5   K×P
41. K–B6

Decisive; but there is still some pretty play.

41.   N–B3
42. K×P   K–Q2
43. K–N7   K–K1
44. K×P   K–B2
45. B–N2   N–N5
46. P–N4!   N–Q6

Hoping for some relief after 20 N—B3, Q—R4 (21 Q×P?, R—Q1, followed by . . . , N—Q6). This is the critical position: how is White to maintain his advantage?

47. **P—N5!**

Elegant play! If 47 . . . , N×B; 48 P—R5 wins.

47.   **P—K4**

A delightful variation would be 47 . . . , N—B5; 48 B—K5, N—R4 (if 48 . . . , N—Q6; 49 B—N3 followed by P—R5 and wins); 49 K—R6, and as soon as Black's Pawn moves are ex-hausted, his King must move, allowing K×P, winning the Knight!

48. **B—B1!**

To prevent . . . , N—B5. If 48 . . . , N×B; 49 P—R5 still wins.

48.		**N—B4**
49.	**P—R5**	**N—K3**
50.	**P×Pch.**	**K—B1**
51.	**P—N7ch.**	Resigns

For if 51 . . . , N×P; 52 B—R3ch., K—B2; 53 P—N6ch., K—B3; 54 B—K7ch., etc. A true master game, finely played and highly enjoyable in all its phases.

GAME 43

Euwe—Alekhine

WORLD CHAMPIONSHIP MATCH, 1937

NIMZOINDIAN DEFENSE

	White	Black
	Euwe	Alekhine
1.	**P—Q4**	**N—KB3**
2.	**P—QB4**	**P—K3**
3.	**N—QB3**	**B—N5**
4.	**N—B3**	**N—K5**

Premature, or at least in-consistent with Black's follow-ing play. 4 . . . , P—QN3, fighting for mastery of White's K4, is a good continuation.

5.	**Q—B2**	**P—Q4**

6.	**P—K3**	**P—QB4**
7.	**B—Q3**	**N—KB3?**

A strange move, and quite inferior to Euwe's suggestion 7 . . . , BP×P; 8 KP×P, N×N; 9 P×N, P×P!; 10 B×BP, B—K2.

7 . . . , Q—R4 (perhaps originally intended by Alek-hine) is simply answered by 8 O—O!, giving Black the op-portunity to go wrong with 8 . . . , B×N; 9 P×B, Q×BP?; 10 B×N!, Q×R; 11 BP×P, and

Black is helpless against the coming B—R3.

8.	BP×P	KP×P
9.	P×P	B×P
10.	O—O	N—B3

Black has lost valuable time, and even castling is a problem. After 10 . . . , O—O; 11 P—K4! is quite formidable, for example: 11 . . . , P×P; 12 N× P, N×N; 13 B×N, with double attack.

11. P—K4!

Now, too, this move is powerful, thanks to the insecure position of Black's King and the vastly superior position of White's forces.

11.   B—K2

White was threatening to win a Pawn by 12 N×P.

Both 11 . . . , N—QN5; 12 B—N5ch., B—Q2; 13 Q—K2 and 11 . . . , P×P; 12 N×P, N×N; 13 B×N, Q—N3; 14 R—K1 are basically hopeless for Black.

12. P—K5   N—KN5?!

Very risky, but Alekhine is understandably reluctant to play the passive 12 . . . , N—Q2.

13. R—K1

Other good moves are 13 Q—K2 and 13 B—KB4.

13.		N—N5
14.	B—N5ch.	K—B1!

Alekhine remains true to his primary object of creating as many complications as possible in order to confuse the issue. After 14 . . . , B—Q2 a likely possibility is 15 Q—B5!, N—QB3; 16 P—K6!, B×P; 17 R×B!, P×R; 18 Q×N, with a winning game.

15.	Q—K2	B—QB4
16.	N—Q1	B—B4

Threatening . . . , N—B7 and thus hoping to keep White occupied. But now White turns his attention to the awkwardly posted King Knight.

17. P—KR3!

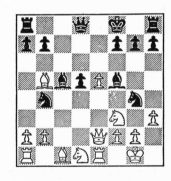

Now it seems that all of Black's sins have caught up with him, for if 17 . . . , N—KR3; 18 B×N, P×B; 19 N—K3!, B×N; 20 Q×B, N—B7; 21 Q×Pch., K—N1; 22 N—R4, winning easily.

The consequences of 17 . . . , N—B7?; 18 P×N are equally bleak.

17.   P—KR4!?

If now 18 P×N, P×P; 19 N—KN5, N—B7; 20 B—KB4, P—N6 and Black's counterplay is very annoying.

18. **B—N5**   **Q—N3**
19. **N—R4!?**

19 P×N, P×P; 20 N—R4 is more incisive, but very taxing for over-the-board play:
a) 20 . . . , B—K5; 21 P—K6!, Q×P; 22 P—R3, N—B7; 23 Q×N, B×Q; 24 R×Q, P×R; 25 R—B1, B×N; 26 N—N6ch. wins.
b) 20 . . . , P—N6; 21 B—K7ch. (simpler than 21 N×B, P×Pch.; 22 N×P, B×Nch.; 23 Q×B, R—R8ch.; 24 K×R, Q×Q; 25 R—KB1, etc.), B×B; 22 N×B, P×Pch.; 23 N×P, B—B4; 24 R—KB1, and wins.

19.   **B—K5**
20. **P×N**   **N—B7**

Alekhine avoids the inadequate lines of the previous note.

21. **N—QB3!**   **N—Q5!!**

21 . . . , N×QR; 22 R×N, P×P, simplifies too much: 23 N—R4, B×Pch.; 24 K—B1!

22. **Q—B1**   **P×P**

Now Black threatens . . . , N—K3 or . . . , P—B3 or . . . , P—N6 or . . . , R—R4.
If White tries to bolster his King's Knight with 23 P—KN3?, then 23 . . . , R×N! 24 P×R, N—B6ch. wins.

23. **N—R4!**   **Q—B2**

Alekhine always dismisses the simple ways: if 23 . . . , Q×B; 24 Q×Q, N×Q; 25 N×B, R—R4; 26 R×B, P×R; 27 N×KP, with an easy win for White.

24. **R×B**

Another way was 24 N×B, Q×N; 25 B—Q3:
a) 25 . . . , N—K3; 26 B—K3, B×B; 27 B×Qch., N×B; 28 R—K2, R×N; 29 Q—B1! and wins.
b) 25 . . . , R—R4; 26 QR—B1, Q—N3; 27 B×B, P×B; 28 B—K3!, R×N; 29 KR—Q1, R—Q1; 30 B—N5, winning.

24.   **P×R**
25. **Q—B4**   **R—B1**

Or 25 . . . , B—N3; 26 P—K6!, N×P; 27 N—N6ch.!, and Black's situation is hopeless.

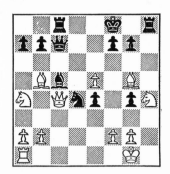

26. **R—QB1!**

At first sight 26 R—Q1 promises a quick win: 26 . . . , N×B; 27 N×B, P—R3 (not 27 . . . , Q×N??; 28 Q×Qch.,

R×Q; 29 R—Q8 mate); 28 R—Q7, etc.

But after 26 R—Q1, Black can play 26 . . . , Q×P!; 27 N×B, Q×N; 28 Q×Qch., R×Q; 29 R×N, R×QB!; 30 R—Q8ch., K—K2; 31 R×R, R×B, and Black has an easy draw in view of the double threat . . . , P—N4 or . . . , R×P.

| 26. | P—QN3 |

Here 26 . . . , Q×P? will not do at all: 27 N×B, Q×B; 28 N—K6ch.!, N×N; 29 Q×Rch., K—K2; 30 R—B7ch.!, K—B3; 31 Q×R, N×R; 32 Q—Q8ch., etc.

| 27. | N×B | P×N |

If 27 . . . , Q×N?; 28 Q×N!

| 28. | B—QR6? |

Very inviting, for if the Rook moves, White has a win with 29 Q×N.

The right way is 28 P—K6!, N×B; 29 Q×N, K—N1; 30 Q—Q7, or 28 . . . , N×P; 29 N—N6ch., winning easily.

| 28. | | Q×P! |
| 29. | B×R | Q×B |

Threatening . . . , Q×N—or . . . , Q×Rch.!

| 30. | Q×QBPch. | Q×Q |
| 31. | R×Q |

White can expect no more than a draw now; hence 31 N—N6ch.! is more convincing.

| 31. | | R×N |
| 32. | R—B4 |

Underestimating Black's resources. 32 B—R6 or 32 R—K5 is an easier way to draw.

| 32. | | N—K7ch. |
| 33. | K—B1 | N—B5 |

Threatening mate!

| 34. | K—N1 | P—N6! |

Now the threat is 35 . . . , R—R8ch.!!; 36 K×R, P×P; 37 R—B1, P—K6; 38 B—R6, P—K7; 39 B×P, N×B; 40 R—Q1, N—N6ch., winning.

| 35. | B—R6! |

If 35 R×P?, N—R6ch. wins. If 35 P×P, N—K7ch.; 36 K—B1 (if 36 K—B2?, P—K6ch.), N×Pch.; 37 K—K1, P—B4, and Black should win.

| 35. | | P×Pch. |
| 36. | K×P | R—R3? |

Time pressure. The right way was 36 . . . , N—Q6ch., maintaining his winning chances.

| 37. | R×P? |

Also pressed for time, Euwe misses 37 R—B8ch.!, K—K2; 38 R—B7ch., and 39 R×RP, with good winning chances. Now a draw is the legitimate outcome.

37.		R×B
38.	R×N	R×P
39.	R—QN4	P—N3
40.	R—N7	K—N2
41.	K—B3	P—N4
42.	P—QN4	K—N3
43.	P—N5	P—B4

44.	P–N6	R–R6ch.
45.	K–B2	P–R3
46.	R–N8	R–QN6
47.	P–N7	K–N2
48.	R–QR8	R×P
49.	R×P	Drawn

This game, with all its flaws, provides an unforgettable portrait of two great masters. There have been few fighters like Alekhine in the history of chess.

GAME 44

Reshevsky—Botvinnik

AVRO TOURNAMENT, 1938

Sammy Reshevsky (born 1911) was taken as a child prodigy to the United States and later became an American citizen. He reappeared in the 1930's as a fully fledged master and rapidly proved himself the strongest player in America. He has had many international tournament successes and won the United States championship in 1936, 1938, 1940, 1942, and 1946.

Mikhail Botvinnik (born 1911) began to win his great reputation in 1931, when he carried off the Russian championship. In a nation of many masters he has consistently shown himself the greatest. His tournament successes include Leningrad, 1934; Moscow, 1935; Nottingham, 1936; and Groningen, 1946. He became world champion in 1948 in a tournament held under F.I.D.E. auspices, and he retained his title in a drawn match with David Bronstein in 1951.

NIMZOINDIAN DEFENSE

	White	Black
	Reshevsky	Botvinnik
1.	P–Q4	N–KB3
2.	P–QB4	P–K3
3.	N–QB3	B–N5
4.	P–K3	O–O
5.	N–K2	P–Q4
6.	P–QR3	B–K2!

Retaining his Bishop pair. The loss of time involved is of slight significance, as White's development of his King side is necessarily a bit cumbersome.

7.	P×P	N×P
8.	N×N	P×N
9.	P–KN3	

Deciding that the pressure of his Bishop on the center will outweigh any weakness of the white squares.

9.		N–Q2
10.	B–N2	N–B3
11.	O–O	B–Q3

A loss of valuable time. He should play . . . , R—K1 and . . . , B—B1 directly.

12.	N—B3	P—B3
13.	P—QN4	P—QR3
14.	R—K1	

This may be superfluous. The immediate 14 P—B3, R—K1; 15 P—K4, P×P; 16 P×P, B—N5; 17 Q—Q2, B—KB1; 18 P—K5 seems quite strong, and explains why Black's 11th move was inexact.

14.		R—K1
15.	B—N2	B—B1
16.	Q—Q3	B—K3
17.	P—B3	N—Q2!

Black's counterplay against the coming advance of the King Pawn is of a high order. For example, after 18 P—K4, P×P; 19 P×P, N—N3, Black's subsequent occupation of QB5 gives him a very promising game.

18.	N—R4	P—QN3!

Threatening to free himself with . . . , P—QB4.

19.	QR—B1	

If 19 P—K4, P×P; 20 P×P, P—QN4!, intending . . . , B—B5 and . . . , P—QR4, when Black's Queen-side initiative is more promising than White's preponderance in the center.

19.		P—QN4!

The time lost by Black in advancing his Queen Knight Pawn will be regained by him when he gets his Knight to QB5. (See White's 23rd move.)

20.	N—B5	N—N3
21.	B—B3	R—R2!
22.	P—K4	N—B5
23.	R—R1	B×N!

Giving up the Bishop pair, and parting with the better Bishop at that. But Black has his reasons.

24.	QP×B	

After 24 NP×B, White's Queen Bishop would still have no scope.

24.		R—Q2!

This explains Black's rather mysterious 21st and 23rd moves: the Rook promises to become active on the Queen file.

25.	Q—Q4	P—B3
26.	P—B4	

White soon finds himself in serious difficulties, but the alternative 26 B—B1, N—K4; 27 B—K2, P×P; 28 Q×KP, B—Q4; 29 Q—KB4, QR—K2 is far from inviting.

26.		P×P!
27.	Q×KP	R—Q6!
28.	QR—B1	R×B!
29.	R×R	B—B2!

Reshevsky has been completely outplayed (if 30 Q—N1?, Q—Q5ch. winning for Black), but in this desperate situation he manages to find a resource.

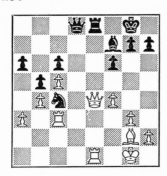

30. R—Q3!?   Q—N1?

The correct move is 30 . . . ,
Q—B1! with these possibilities:

a) 31 KR—Q1, R×Q; 32
B×R, B—Q4!; 33 B×Bch., P×
B; 34 R×P, Q—N5!, and
White's attack is over.

b) 31 Q×P, R×Rch.; 32
K—B2, R—K1; 33 Q×Q, R×Q;
34 B—N7, R—N1, and wins.

31. R/K1—Q1! R×Q
32. B×R

Or 32 R—Q8ch., R—K1, and
Black is a piece to the good
without complications.

32.   Q—KB1

32 . . . , B—Q4 will not do
because of 33 B×Bch., P×B;
34 R×P, K—B2; 35 R—Q8,
and Black's Queen is lost.

The amount of pressure un-
leashed by White is astonishing, considering that he has
only two Rooks for Queen
and Knight.

33. R—Q8   B—K1
34. R—K1!

Now the threat is 35 R×B!
Reshevsky prefers to rely on
the diabolical Rooks rather
than steer into a good ending
with two pieces for Rook and
Pawn by means of 34 B×P,
B×B; 35 R×Qch., K×R, etc.

34.   K—B2
35. B×RP

In view of the threatened
36 R/Q8×B, Q×R; 37 B—
N6ch., Black now sees himself
forced to return the extra
piece; leaving White with two
Rooks for the Queen.

35.   N—K4

If instead 35 . . . , Q—R1;
36 B—B5!, Q—R4; 37 P—N4,
and wins.

36. P×N   Q—R1

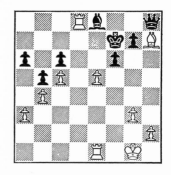

37. B—B2?

There was an easy win with
37 P×P!, Q×B; 38 P×P, Q×P;
39 R/Q8×B. The power of
White's co-operating Rooks,
the strength of his passed
Pawns, and the weakness of

Black's Pawns—all these add up to victory.

37.   K—K2
38. R—B8?

Another slip. 38 R—N8! (or 38 R—R8!) still wins.

38.   P—B4!

To close the King file.

39. B×P   Q—R4
40. P—N4?

There is still a winning chance with 40 B—K4 (if then 40 . . . , Q×P??; 41 R×Bch.! wins nicely).

40.   Q—N4!

With his Rook on QN8 (or QR8) White could now play 41 R—N7ch. (or 41 R—R7ch.), K—Q1; 42 R—Q1ch.; or 41 . . . , K—B1; 42 B—K6!, and wins.

41. R—B7ch.   K—Q1

With his Rook *en prise,* White has no time for R—Q1ch. This is the finesse that Reshevsky missed.

42. R—B8ch.

42 R—R7 is not decisive, as Black has the resource 42 . . . , Q—Q7!

42.   K—K2
43. P—K6   P—N3!

An important feature of the defense.

44. R—B7ch.   K—Q1
45. R—Q7ch.!

A last desperate attempt to win, based on the passed King Pawn.

45.   K—B1!

Not 45 . . . , B×R?; 46 P—K7ch., K—B2; 47 B×B, and wins.

Or if 45 . . . , B×R?; 46 P—K7ch., Q×P; 47 R×Q, K×R; 48 B×B, K×B; 49 P—KR4, with a won ending.

46. P—K7   P×B
47. R—Q8ch.   K—B2
48. R×B   Q×Pch.
49. K—R1   Q—B6ch.
50. K—N1   Q—N5ch.
      Drawn

White loses a Rook if he tries to evade the checks.

GAME 45

Ulvestad—Reinfeld

VENTNOR CITY, 1939

Olaf Ulvestad is one of the most interesting players on the American scene. His play bristles with original ideas.
Fred Reinfeld (born 1910) is a noted writer on chess.

QUEEN'S GAMBIT
DECLINED
(in effect)

White	Black
Ulvestad	Reinfeld
1. N—KB3	N—KB3
2. P—B4	P—K3
3. P—QN3	P—Q4
4. B—N2	P—B4
5. P—K3	N—B3
6. P—Q4	BP×P

Beginning a series of Pawn exchanges in order to leave White with definitive Pawn weaknesses in the center. In addition, he prepares for . . . , B—N5ch., as simplification goes hand in hand with the creation of organic weaknesses.

7. KP×P	P×P
8. B×P	B—N5ch.
9. K—K2!?	

Rather than simplify, Ulvestad resolutely chances the possibility that his King may get into trouble.

9.	N—Q4
10. Q—QB1	O—O
11. R—Q1	B—Q2

| 12. P—QR3 | B—Q3 |
| 13. N—B3 | R—B1 |

Now White must not try to win a Pawn on Q5, as Black would win the Queen by an eventual . . . , N×Pch.

| 14. N—K4 | B—B5 |
| 15. Q—N1 | P—B4 |

15 . . . , N—R4 is more solid. But Black wants to play for attack, and consequently ignores the possibility of creating troublesome Pawn weaknesses.

16. N—B5	N—R4
17. P—N3	B—Q3
18. Q—Q3	P—QN4?!

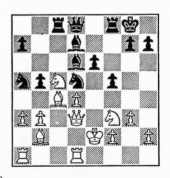

A further reckless weakening in his quest for attack. He anticipates 19 N×B, P×B!; 20 P×P, N×P!; 21 N×R, N×B, etc.—or 19 B×P, B×B; 20 Q×B, R—N1; 21 Q—Q7, Q×Q!; 22 N×Q, R×P, with a promising formation for Black in either event.

| 19. | B×N! | P×B |
| 20. | QR—B1 | P—B5! |

White's simple positional treatment promises to be extremely effective. With a bad Pawn position and a Knight out of play, Black plays for the opening of the King Bishop file, augmented, if possible, by the formidable pin . . . , B—KN5.

| 21. | N×B | Q×N |
| 22. | N—K5 | B×N? |

In order to be able to play . . . , Q—N5ch. But 22 . . . , QR—K1 serves the same purpose and strengthens the attack considerably. The coming frontal attack on the Queen Pawn, as well as the passed Pawn status of White's King Pawn, will make Black's life miserable.

23.	P×B	R×R
24.	R×R	P×P
25.	RP×P	Q—N5ch.

If now 26 K—B1, Q—K5, with satisfactory counter-chances. Ulvestad characteristically selects the riskiest method.

26.	P—B3	Q×P
27.	Q×Pch.	K—R1
28.	Q—B7!	

Threatening mate; and Black has thirteen moves to make in a matter of seconds!

| 28. | | Q—N7ch. |
| 29. | K—K3 | |

Playing for a win, White must bring his King out in the open.

| 29. | | Q—N4ch. |
| 30. | K—B2 | |

On 30 K—K4, it would be bad to continue 30 . . . , Q—N3ch.?, which leads to a lost ending. But 30 . . . , Q—Q1!; 31 R—Q1!, Q—R1ch.!; 32 Q—Q5, Q—B1! keeps Black's attack going.

30.		Q—Q7ch.
31.	K—N3	Q—N4ch.
32.	K—R3	

No perpetual check! And if 32 . . . , Q—R3ch.?; 33 K—N4!, Q—N3ch.; 34 Q×Q, and the ending is lost for Black.

32.		Q—Q1
33.	R—Q1!	Q—B1ch.
34.	Q—Q7	R×Pch.
35.	K—N4	Q—KB1

Black has managed to obtain enough counterplay for a draw.

36.	Q—Q8!	R—B5ch.
37.	K—R5	R—B4ch.
38.	K—N4	R—B5ch.
39.	K—R5	R—B4ch.
40.	K—N4	

40.   P—R4ch.?!

Instead of taking the draw,
Black decides to play on, as
this is the last move for the
time control.

41. K—R4

The perpetual check is gone,
and with ample time at his
disposal, Black realizes that
he has apparently played himself into a lost game: his
Knight is attacked and has
been out of the game for
twenty-five moves; White's
passed Pawn looks more formidable than ever; it is difficult to see what Black can do

in the face of the threatened
Q×Qch., followed by R—Q7
and P—K6.

Note, by the way, that 41
. . . , R—B5ch.? will not do:
42 K×P!, R—B4ch.; 43 K—
N6!, etc.

41.   K—N1!!

This far from obvious move
holds everything. The threat
against Black's Knight turns
out to be bogus, for if 42 Q×
N??, R—B5ch.; 43 K—N3, R—
N5ch., or 43 K—R3, Q—B4ch.
and in either event Black
forces mate!

42. P—K6   N—B3!

With the centralization of
Black's King and Knight, the
end game is shorn of its
terrors.

43. Q×Qch.   K×Q
44. R—Q7   K—K1!
45. R×NP   N—Q1
46. R×P   N×P
      Drawn

Both players were awarded
a special prize for this game.

Rojahn—Czerniak

INTERNATIONAL TEAM TOURNAMENT, BUENOS AIRES, 1939

E. Rojahn is one of the leading Norwegian players.

M. Czerniak, perhaps the outstanding master of Israel's chess-loving community, made a great name for himself as an annotator and writer on the game during his stay in Argentina. He took first prize in the Vienna tournament of 1951.

NIMZOVICH DEFENSE

White	Black
Rojahn	Czerniak
1. P–K4	N–QB3
2. P–Q4	P–Q4
3. P–K5	B–B4
4. P–KN4?!	

This unusual move gives the game a wild character that becomes more intense as play continues.

4.	B–N3
5. N–KR3	P–K3
6. N–B4	B–K5
7. R–N1	N–R3
8. B–K3	B–K2
9. N–Q2	

Getting rid of the obstreperous Bishop.

9.	B–R5
10. N×B	P×N
11. B–N2	Q–K2

Calmly ignoring the threat to his King Pawn—not that he can do much about it—and preparing to castle Queen side.

12. B×P	N×KP!?

For if 13 P×N, Q–N5ch., and 14 . . . , Q×B with advantage.

13. P–N5	

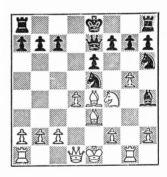

13.	N–B5!

If 13 . . . , N–B4?; 14 B×N wins a piece. And if 13 . . . , B×P?; 14 R×B!, Q×R; 15 P×N.

14. P×N	N×B
15. P×P!?	

Stronger was 15 Q–Q3!, P–KN4; 16 N–R5, N–B4; 17

161

162   ROJAHN—CZERNIAK

B×N, P×Bch.; 18 Q—K2, and
White has the better ending.

| 15. | B×Pch.! |

If now 16 K×B??, Black
takes the Queen *with check*.

16.	K—K2!	KR—N1
17.	Q—Q3	B×R
18.	Q—N5ch.!

The only chance: if 18 R×B,
N—Q4!

| 18. | P—B3 |

On other moves, 19 Q×P
wins.

| 19. | B×Pch.! | K—Q1! |
| 20. | B×P |

Black is momentarily a
Rook ahead but finds himself
in great difficulties. An inter-
esting defense is 20 . . . , N—
B4; 21 Q—R5ch., Q—B2; 22
Q×Qch., K×Q; 23 B×R, B×
RP; 24 N—R5!, when White
should draw.

| 20. | N×P?! |

Threatening 21 . . . , N×
Pch., as well as 21 . . . , N×R.
20 . . . , R—N1 seems ade-
quate, as after 21 Q—R5ch.,
Q—B2; 22 Q—N5ch., K—K1,
White has no time for 23 N—
R5 because of 23 . . . , Q×
BPch. winning.

21. Q—R5ch.

Here White offered a draw
(!), which Black of course
refused.

21.		Q—B2
22.	N×Pch.!!	P×N
23.	Q—N5ch.	Q—K2

If 23 . . . , K—K1; 24 Q—
R5ch., or 23 . . . , K—Q2; 24
Q—N5ch.

24. Q—R5ch.

Whereupon Black accepted
the draw, after discovering
that he must actually *lose* unless he continues interposing
the Queen.

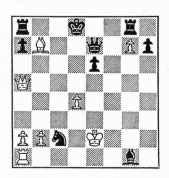

If 24 . . . , K—K1; 25 B—
B6ch., K—B2; 26 R—B1ch.,
K×P; 27 R×Bch., K—R1; 28
Q—K5ch., R—N2; 29 B×R,
and White will win the end-
ing.
If 24 . . . , K—Q2; 25 Q—
N5ch., K—B2; 26 R—QB1, B×
QP; 27 R×Nch., K—N1; 28
R—B8ch.!!, R×R; 29 B×KR
dis. ch.!!, and the twice-at-
tacked passed Pawn queens!
A thrilling game.

Nyman—Sköld

STOCKHOLM, 1943

S. Nyman and K. Sköld are two leading Swedish players.

RUY LOPEZ

	White	Black
	Nyman	Sköld
1.	P–K4	P–K4
2.	N–KB3	N–QB3
3.	B–N5	P–QR3
4.	B–R4	N–B3
5.	O–O	N×P

This move is always an indication that Black means to have a lively game.

6.	P–Q4	P–QN4
7.	B–N3	P–Q4
8.	P×P	B–K3
9.	P–QR4!?	N–R4!
10.	N–Q4	N×B
11.	P×N	P×P?

Now Black gets his complications, but in a highly unappetizing form. Correct is 11 . . . , P–N5! with a good game.

12.	P–QN4!	P–QB4?!

Perhaps the abject 12 . . . , P–KR4 (not 12 . . . , B×P?; 13 Q×Pch.) is best to save his menaced Knight.

13.	N×B	P×N
14.	P–B3!	N–N4
15.	Q×Pch.	K–B2

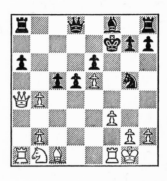

16.	P–N5?	

White intends to queen this Pawn, and he will succeed—but he will resign at once! Correct is 16 P–R4, P–R3; 17 P×N, RP×P; 18 B–K3, and Black does not have compensation for his piece.

16.		P–B5?!

Black is likewise more daring than sound, disdaining to save his menaced Knight.

17.	P–R4	B–B4ch.
18.	K–R2	P–R3
19.	P×P?	

After 19 P×N, P×P dis. ch.; 20 K–N3, Black has no good continuation of the attack.

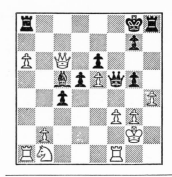

19.   **K—N1!!**

The beginning of an amazing plan: if 20 P×N, P×Pch.; 21 K—N3, P—N5!, wins.

20. **P—KN3**   **Q—KB1!!**

Threatening 21 . . . , Q—B4, as well as 21 . . . , N×Pch.

21. **K—N2**

If 21 P×N, P×P dis. ch.; 22 K—N2, Q—B4; 23 R—R1, R× R; 24 K×R, Q—R6 mate—or 23 P—KN4, Q—R2, forcing mate. White's undeveloped Queen side is a terrible handicap.

21.   **Q—B4!**
22. **B×N**   **P×B**

So he has an open King Rook file after all; but White's last move was as good as forced.

23. **Q—B6!?**

This is the move on which White relied to give him a won game. But Black has seen farther ahead!

[*See diagram in next column.*]

23.   **P×P!!**

White is lost! If 24 Q×B, P×P; 25 R—R1 (if 25 K×P, Q—N4ch.; 26 K—B2, R—R7ch.; 27 K—K1, Q—B8 mate. Note

the undeveloped Knight!), R×R; 26 K×R, Q—R6ch.; 27 K—N1, Q—R7ch.; 28 K—B1, P—N7ch., queening and winning White's Queen!

If 24 P—KN4, P—R6ch. wins very quickly.

24. **Q×Rch.**   **K—R2**
25. **Q×Rch.**   **K×Q**
26. **P—R7**

Expecting 26 . . . , B×P when White will at least draw.

26.   **Q—N4!!**

It is more important for Black to retain his Bishop than to prevent the Pawn promotion.

27. **P—R8(Q)ch.** **K—R2**
        Resigns!

There is no way to stop mate! If 28 P—KN4, Q—B5, etc.

GAME 48

Euwe—Bisguier

NEW YORK, 1948–49

Arthur Bisguier, the most brilliant of the younger American masters, won the United States Open Championship in 1950 at the age of twenty-two.

QUEEN'S GAMBIT
DECLINED

White	Black
Euwe	Bisguier
1. P–Q4	P–Q4
2. P–QB4	P–QB3
3. N–KB3	P–K3
4. N–B3	N–B3
5. B–N5	P–KR3
6. B×N	Q×B

In surrendering the Bishop pair, White hopes to get a compensating advantage in space. Black, on the other hand, looks forward to the time when he will be able to break out of his cramped position.

7. Q–N3	N–Q2
8. P–K4	P×KP
9. N×P	Q–B5
10. B–Q3	N–B3
11. N×Nch.	P×N?!

Bisguier does not mind the weakening of his Pawn position and the insecure position of his King, so long as he opens the King Knight file for attacking purposes.

| 12. O–O | KR–N1 |

13. B–K2	P–N3
14. KR–K1	Q–B2
15. P–B5!	B–QN2
16. B–B4!	

The danger to Black's King has become very real, and 17 B×P is already threatened. 16 . . . , O–O–O? will not do because of 17 B×Pch.!

16.	B–K2
17. P×P	P×P
18. QR–B1	Q–Q1

Preventing 19 P–Q5!

| 19. Q–K3 | R–R1 |

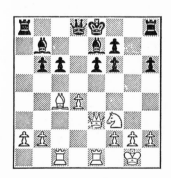

20. B×P?!

Enterprising, but Black is

165

not without resources. 20 KR—Q1 is more solid.

| 20. | P×B |
| 21. | Q×KP | K—B1 |

He has to do something about the menace of N—R4—B5.

| 22. | N—R4 | KR—N1 |
| 23. | N—B5 |

His best course seems 23 Q—K3, although Black can defend himself with 23 . . . , R—R4!; 24 Q×Pch., K—B2.

23.	B—N5!
24.	N×P	R—N2
25.	R—K3!?

From this point on, the course of the game is particularly tense. Black's most effective reply is 25 . . . , P—QB4!; 26 R—KN3, B—Q4!

25.	B—Q7!?
26.	R—KB3	B—N4
27.	N—B5!

27 P—KR4 is met by 27 . . . , P—QB4!

| 27. | B×R!? |

Good enough, but there is a much simpler defense in 27 . . . , R—KR2!

| 28. | R—KR3! |

White's last move (threatening mate in two) is apparently conclusive; for if 28 . . . , KR—N1?; 29 R—R7 decides.

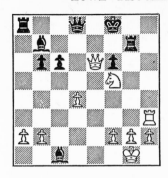

| 28. | R×Pch.!! |

With a Rook and Bishop ahead, Black can afford to indulge in such pleasantries. Note that the Rook must be captured:

a) 29 K—R1??, KR—N1!!; 30 R—R7, Q—Q4ch., and wins.

b) 29 K—B1??, KR—N1!!; 30 R—R7, B—R3ch.; 31 K—K1, R—N8 mate!

29.	K×R	Q—Q4ch.
30.	Q×Q	P×Q
31.	R—R7!!

Black must now return the extra piece, for if 31 . . . , R—R2; 32 P—KR4! (stronger than 32 N—Q6, B×P), and the passed Pawn continues to march.

Other moves are even worse for Black: 31 . . . , R—N1? (or 31 . . . , B—QR3?); 32 R—R8ch.—or 31 . . . , B—B3; 32 R—B7.

| 31. | R×P? |

Correct is 31 . . . , B—B1!; 32 R—R8ch., K—B2; 33 R×B,

R×R; 34 N–Q6ch., K–K3; 35 N×R, B×P; 36 N–R7 (not 36 N×P??, B×P), and the ending is a draw.

32.	R×B	R×P
33.	P–R4!	B–Q7
34.	K–B1!	R–N8ch.
35.	K–K2	B–B6

Also hopeless is 35 . . . , B–B5; 36 P–R5, R–KR8; 37 P–R6, B×P; 38 R–KR7, etc.

| 36. | P–R5 | P–N4 |

| 37. | P–R6 | K–N1 |
| 38. | N–K7ch. | K–R2 |

Loses a piece, but if 38 . . . , K–B1; 39 N–N6ch. wins right off.

| 39. | N×P dis. ch. | K×P |
| 40. | N×B | Resigns |

An unusually attractive game, in which both players have produced delightfully imaginative chess.

GAME 49

Barden–O'Kelly

HASTINGS, 1948–49

L. W. Barden is a young English player who is particularly noted for his authoritative articles on opening play.

Alberic O'Kelly de Galway, a Belgian master of Irish descent, worthily carries on the tradition of his great countryman Colle. Profiting by his association with the famous Akiba Rubinstein, O'Kelly has won many high prizes in tournament play.

SICILIAN DEFENSE

	White	Black
	Barden	O'Kelly
1.	P–K4	P–QB4
2.	N–KB3	P–Q3
3.	P–Q4	P×P
4.	N×P	N–KB3
5.	N–QB3	P–QR3
6.	P–B4	P–K3

By transposition, O'Kelly has reached the Scheveningen Defense, a line against which he has achieved some notable successes with the White pieces.

7.	B–K3	Q–B2
8.	B–K2	N–B3
9.	O–O	B–Q2
10.	Q–K1	N×N

If Black plays 10 . . . , B–K2, then 11 Q–N3 exposes him to a strong attack. So he tries a different way.

| 11. | B×N | B–B3 |
| 12. | B–B3 | N–Q2 |

To take the sting out of White's contemplated P—K5.

13. **N—Q5!**

A clever move. If 13 . . . , P×N; 14 P×P dis. ch. recovers the piece advantageously.

13.	**B×N**
14. **P×B**	**P—K4**
15. **B—N4!**	**P—B3**

White's Bishops are powerful, making Black's defense exceedingly onerous.

16. **R—Q1**   **B—K2**

O'Kelly tries to get his pieces in play, as 16 . . . , Q×P; 17 B×Nch., K×B; 18 R—B1, Q—R5; 19 B—N6 is anything but inviting.

17. **B—QB3**   **N—B4**

17 . . . , O—O? does not help at all, as after 18 B—K6ch., K—R1; 19 P—B5!, White threatens a mating attack with R—Q3—R3, etc.

| *18.* **P×P** | **QP×P** |
| *19.* **B—R5ch.** | **P—N3** |
| *20.* **P—Q6!** |

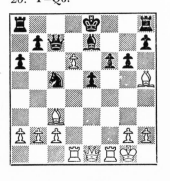

Black's position seems to be bursting at the seams. If 20 . . . , B×P; 21 R×P!, B—K2; 22 B×P, Q—B1; 23 R×NP!, P×R; 24 B×Pch., K—B1; 25 Q—B2ch., forcing mate.

20.   **Q—N3!**

With the nasty threat of 21 . . . , N—Q6 dis. ch.

21. **Q—K3**   **B—Q1!**

He shuns 21 . . . , P×B; 22 P×B, K×P; 23 B—Q4, QR—QB1; 24 P—QN4!, Q×P; 25 R×P!, K×R; 26 Q×Pch., forcing mate.

22. **B—Q4!**   **N—Q2!**

If 22 . . . , QR—B1?; 23 P—Q7ch.! wins on the spot!
    Black's Knight move is a gallant try, although his game is still lost.

23. **R×P!!**

Beautiful play. His Bishop is still left *en prise,* while 23 . . . , B×R or 23 . . . , N×R permits 24 B×Q in reply.

23.   **Q—R4**

Not 23 . . . , P×B; 24 R—K6ch., K—B2; 25 R—K7ch., and White has a winning attack.

24. **R—K6ch.?!**

More conclusive is 24 P—QN4!, Q×P; 25 B×P, leaving Black's King helpless.

24.   **K—B2**

With only four minutes left

for twelve moves, White has a task that is far from easy!

25.	Q–QN3!	K–N2
26.	Q×P	KP×B
27.	Q×Nch.	K–R3
28.	B–B3	QR–N1
29.	R–K4	R–KB1
30.	QR×P!	

Hoping to provoke 30 . . . , B–N3?, when 31 R–R4ch., K–N4; 32 Q–K7ch. wins quickly.

| 30. | | R–B5!? |

Resourceful to the end. With only a few seconds to go, White sees that 31 R×R?? allows 31 . . . , Q–K8 mate—but he fails to find the win.

[*See diagram in next column.*]

31. P–KR3?

31 P–QN4!, R×R; 32 P×

Q wins for White without much trouble.

31.		R×R
32.	R×R	R×P
33.	Q–KB7?	Q–B4ch.
34.	K–R2	Q×Pch.
35.	P–N3	R×Pch.
36.	B–N2	R–B2
	Drawn	

The effects of Barden's time pressure were unfortunate, but O'Kelly fully earned his half point!

GAME 50

Matanovich–Rossolimo

STAUNTON CENTENARY TOURNAMENT, 1951

Aleksandar Matanovich (born 1930) made his debut in Yugoslav chess at a very early age. He is one of that country's finest players and seems assured of a brilliant future in international chess.

Nicholas Rossolimo was born in Russia of Greek parentage and has lived most of his life in Paris. He has represented France in many postwar tournaments, with striking success.

RUY LOPEZ

White	Black
Matanovich	Rossolimo
1. P–K4	P–K4
2. N–KB3	N–QB3
3. B–N5	P–QR3
4. B–R4	N–B3
5. O–O	B–K2
6. R–K1	P–QN4
7. B–N3	P–Q3
8. P–B3	B–N5

A somewhat unusual move in this familiar form of the Lopez. White's most exact reply is 9 P–Q3 and if 9 . . . , O–O; 10 P–KR3.

9. P–KR3

By driving off the Bishop *before* Black castles, White exposes himself to a potential counterattack.

9.	B–R4
10. P–Q3	P–R3!

Intending to exploit White's 9th move by . . . , P–N4 and . . . , P–KN5. Matan-

ovich extricates himself from this difficulty rather well.

11. P–N4	B–N3
12. N–R4	Q–Q2

The counterthrust 12 . . . , P–KR4 is parried by 13 N× B, P×N; 14 P–N5.

13. Q–B3	N–QR4
14. B–B2	N–R2
15. N–B5	

Here or earlier, N×B only succeeds in giving Black an open King Bishop file.

15.	B–B3
16. N–Q2	P–R4!

Well timed, as White cannot reply P–N5.

17. N–B1	P×P
18. Q×P!	

This gives White a much more active game than would result from the more orthodox 18 P×P, when Black replies 18 . . . , K–B1! preparing . . . , N–N4.

170

18.	N–B3
19.	N/B1–N3	N–B1
20.	P–QR4	QR–N1

Better than 20 . . . , P–N5;
21 P–R5! preparing 22 B–R4.

| 21. | P×P | P×P |
| 22. | R–R6 |

A familiar maneuver in this opening. The Rook on the open Queen Rook file always manages to play an important role in positions of this character.

22.		N–K3
23.	P–N4	K–B1
24.	B–N3

The Bishop is effectively posted here.

| 24. | | N/B3–Q1 |

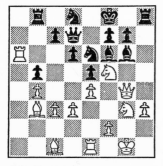

25. P–Q4!

Having posted his pieces advantageously, White now sacrifices two Pawns in order to exploit his superior mobility.

| 25. | | P×P |

26.	P–KB4!	P×P
27.	P–K5!	QP×P
28.	P×P	B–K2
29.	R–Q1!	Q–K1
30.	R–KB1!

Black has been driven into a very cramped position, and the pressure on his KB2 forces him into a very critical situation. There is a direct threat of 31 B×N, N×B; 32 R×N!, P×R; 33 N–Q6 dis. ch., winning the Queen.

| 30. | | R–N3 |
| 31. | R×R |

Intending to answer 31 . . . , P×R; 32 Q×B!, P×Q; 33 N–Q6 dis. ch., N–B2; 34 N×N!, and if 34 . . . , Q×N; 35 B×N!

| 31. | | B×N! |
| 32. | N×B! |

Avoiding 32 Q×B, P×R; 33 B×N, N×B; 34 Q×N??, B–B4ch., and Black wins the Queen!

| 32. | | P×R |
| 33. | R–B3 | Q–B3 |

Black clings like grim death to the passed Pawn.

34.	R–N3	P–N3
35.	N×B	K×N
36.	B–N5ch.	K–K1

Better than 36 . . . , N×B; 37 Q×Nch., K–K1; 38 P–K6!, and Black's King is in greater danger than ever.

| 37. | B–B6 | R–R4 |

38.	Q–Q1	R–B4
39.	R–Q3	Q–B2
40.	Q–QB1?	

Relaxing his grip. 40 Q–B2 is much stronger, and practically forces Black to give up the exchange.

| 40. | | N–B5! |

Rossolimo plays with astonishing tenacity and resourcefulness. He immediately puts his finger on the weakness created by White's last move. The threat is now . . . , N–K7ch.

| 41. | R–K3 | N/Q1–K3 |
| 42. | B–B2 | N–Q5! |

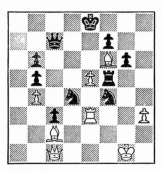

White seems lost, for if 43 B–Q3, N×B wins because of the threat . . . , N–K7ch. And if 43 Q–Q1, Q–N2!; 44 B–K4, P–B7!, and Black must win.

Yet Black's terrible threat of 43 . . . , N–K7ch. can be met! White's correct course is 43 Q–R3!!, N×B; 44 Q–R8ch., K–Q2; 45 R–Q3ch.!!, N×R; 46 Q–Q5ch., and

White has a draw by perpetual check!

| 43. | Q–R1? | |

But this loses because of a tricky point unearthed by Rossolimo.

43.		N/B5–K7ch.
44.	K–N2	Q–N2ch.!
45.	B–K4	N–B7!!
46.	B×Q	

Or 46 R×N, Q×Bch.; 47 R×Q, N×Q, winning easily; for if 48 R–Q4, R×B; 49 P×R, P–B7; 50 R–K4ch., K–Q1; 51 R–K1, N–N6.

| 46. | | N×Rch.! |

If White's Queen were at QR3, he could now play 47 K–R2!, forcing Black to take a draw by 47 . . . , R–B7ch.; 48 K–R1, R–B8ch., etc.

| 47. | K–R1 | |

Whereas if now 47 K–R2, R–B7ch.; 48 K–R1, R–B8ch. with the text continuation!

| 47. | | R–B8ch. |
| 48. | Q×R | N×Q |

Threatening 49 . . . , P–B7. So in essence Black's magnificent counterattack amounts to a simplifying transaction to utilize the passed Pawn.

| 49. | B–B6ch. | K–B1 |
| 50. | B×P | P–B7? |

Not the quickest way. More forcing is 50 . . . , N/B8–N6ch.; 51 K–R2, N–K5!; 52 B–Q3, N×B; 53 P×N, N–Q5, when White will have to give up his Bishop for the terrible Pawn.

The following end game, while somewhat lengthy, is comparatively easy.

51.	B–N5!	N/B8–N6ch.
52.	K–N2	N–K5
53.	B–R6ch.!	K–K2
54.	B–Q3!	

Not 54 B×N??, P–N4!

54.		P–B8(Q)
55.	B×Q	N×B
56.	B×N	N–R7

The state of material equality is deceptive: White's Pawns are ragged, and he must incur some loss.

| 57. | P–N5 | N–B6 |
| 58. | B–B6 | K–K3 |

| 59. | K–B3 | K×P |
| 60. | B–K8 | K–K3 |

The Bishop will soon be in trouble.

61.	K–B4	N–Q4ch.
62.	K–N5	N–B2
63.	B–B6	K–K4
64.	P–R4	N–K3ch.
65.	K–N4	N–Q5
66.	B–K8	K–K3

The Bishop is trapped!

67.	K–B4	K–K2
68.	K–K4	K×B
69.	K×N	P–B3
	Resigns	

Perhaps the most remarkable feature of this thrilling struggle was Rossolimo's wizardry in maneuvering his Knights.

Index of Openings

Alekhine Defense, 110, 130

Center Game, 96

Dutch Defense, 144

English Opening, 106

Evans Gambit, 34, 51

Falkbeer Counter Gambit, 63

French Defense, 45

Giuoco Piano, 19, 38

Kieseritzky Gambit, 22

King's Bishop's Opening, 11

King's Gambit, 76

King's Indian Defense, 123, 137

Nimzoindian Defense, 116, 150, 154

Nimzovich Defense, 161

Petroff Defense, 57

Ponziani Opening, 112

Queen's Gambit, 15

Queen's Gambit Declined, 54, 60, 67, 85, 89, 103, 120, 126, 158, 165

Queen's Pawn Game, 42, 133

Ruy Lopez, 25, 29, 32, 48, 70, 73, 81, 100, 163, 170

Scotch Game, 140

Sicilian Defense, 78, 93, 147, 167

#1239557.